A Horse of a Different Color

A Horse of a Different Color

Television's Treatment Of Jesse Jackson's 1984 Presidential Campaign

C. Anthony Broh

 ®

Joint Center for Political Studies
Washington, D.C.
1987

The Joint Center for Political Studies is a national non-profit institution that conducts research on public policy issues of special concern to black Americans and promotes informed and effective involvement of blacks in the governmental process. Founded in 1970, the Joint Center provides independent and nonpartisan analyses through research, publication, and outreach programs.

Opinions expressed in Joint Center publications are those of the authors and do not necessarily reflect the views of the other staff, officers, or governors of the Joint Center or of the organizations supporting the Center and its research.

We gratefully acknowledge the support of the Ford Foundation and the Rockefeller Foundation, which helped make this publication possible.

Library of Congress Cataloging-in-Publication Data

Broh, C. Anthony.
   A horse of a different color.

   Bibliography: p.
   1. Television in politics—United States.
2. Presidents—United States—Election—1984.
3. Jackson, Jesse, 1941-   I. Title.
HE8700.76.U6B76   1987   324.7'3'0973   87-2869

ISBN 0-941410-54-4

1301 Pennsylvania Ave., N.W.
Suite 400
Washington, D.C. 20004

To Eleanor and Jennifer

*N*ow that's a horse of a different color.

L. FRANK BAUM, *The Wizard of Oz*

*J*esse Jackson demonstrated that he did not—would not—accept his place simply as a black, that he would be regarded as a serious national candidate.

KENNETH B. CLARK, *Washington Post*, **July 6, 1986**

CONTENTS

LIST OF FIGURES

FOREWORD

The success of candidates for public office is greatly influenced by the type of media coverage their campaigns receive, and particularly by coverage from television news. It is vital, therefore, for scholars to examine the way television covers political races. Although a growing number of scholars are doing so, few—if any—have looked at how TV affects the electoral prospects of minority office-seekers.

Into this vacuum comes C. Anthony Broh's *A Horse of a Different Color: Television's Treatment of Jesse Jackson's 1984 Presidential Campaign.* Broh, a political scientist, analyzes more than 2,000 network news programs that were broadcast about the Democratic presidential hopefuls during the nine months before the Democratic national convention in July 1984. Of the five Democrats discussed in the programs and studied by Broh, four were white males; the other was a black male—Jesse Jackson, who captured the nation's attention by his presence in the campaign, even though he had less success capturing the nation's votes.

Jackson's "star quality" (his telegenic presence) and the historic nature of his quest ensured that his campaign would be covered on TV, but the question Broh addresses is how the coverage given to Jackson compared with the coverage given to his white competitors. Did television distinguish Jackson from the rest? If so, in what way(s) and to what extent? Further, did television by its coverage help or hurt Jackson's electoral chances?

To reach his answers, Broh devises a scheme for classifying the elements of TV news coverage in a presidential primary campaign. He sets forth a framework within which election news coverage can be broken down into various categories that can then be analyzed and compared. Indeed, independent of Broh's conclusions, his framework itself has great value as a tool for analyzing media coverage of *any* nominating or presidential campaign. Moreover, Broh shows how his framework derives from a broad range of political science research.

The conclusion Broh reaches is that Jackson was both helped and hurt by the TV treatment he received. He was helped because the media recognized his right to run and to be taken seriously as a candidate. He was hurt because, as a black man, he was thought unable to win—and in "horse-race journalism," a candidate who is thought to have no chance of winning the grand prize, who cannot be viewed as a front runner, a contender, or even a long shot, is treated as "a horse of a different color." Thus, television presented Jackson's candidacy in terms different from the terms in which it presented the candidacies of Alan Cranston, John Glenn, Gary Hart, or Walter Mondale, all of whom were white and whose chances of winning were therefore seen as greater than zero.

In an epilogue, Broh reflects on the lessons of his research for other blacks seeking national office.

This research was commissioned by the Joint Center for Political Studies, and the author's preliminary findings were presented at a conference the Center sponsored in April 1985 to analyze the 1984 elections.

The Center extends thanks to the following people for their contributions to the monograph: F. Christopher Arterton, Thomas E. Cavanagh, Jennifer L. Hochschild, Gary Imhoff, and Milton M. Morris, who commented on early drafts, and Jane E. Lewin, who edited the manuscript.

Eddie N. Williams

1. CONTEXT: JACKSON'S CANDIDACY, TELEVISION'S ROLES

The year 1984 should be remembered for a presidential election that was important to the elderly, to women, and to blacks. None of the three groups gained many seats among the elected, nor were they successful in getting their issues on the political agenda. But one person from each group played a significant role in the presidential election and the preliminaries leading up to it. Ronald Reagan, running for reelection, was the oldest person ever to become a candidate for president. Geraldine Ferraro, the Democratic candidate for vice president, was the first woman ever to be on a major-party ticket. And Jesse Jackson, a black man and the subject of this study, campaigned to become the Democratic candidate for president.

Jesse Jackson was not the first black to seek the presidency. In 1972, Representative Shirley Chisholm had run for the Democratic nomination, and four years earlier two blacks had campaigned for third-party nominations: political satirist Dick Gregory, with the Peace and Freedom party in a campaign that had national visibility, and *Soul on Ice* author Eldridge Cleaver, with the Black Panther party. But Jackson's campaign was distinguished from those of his predecessors both by the level of support it received within the Democratic party and by the seriousness with which it was covered by the national media.

In contrast to Shirley Chisholm or the two third-party candidates, Jackson was considered an important force in party politics. Unlike Chisholm, he won a few Democratic party primaries and caucuses (the District of Columbia, Louisiana, and Puerto Rico). Unlike Gregory or Cleaver, he campaigned not merely to make a symbolic statement or ideological gesture or to become a historic "first." Jesse Jackson's campaign was a serious effort to be nominated by the Democratic party with a view to being elected president of the United States, and in that

Jackson's campaign was distinguished from those of his [black] predecessors both by the level of support it received within the Democratic party and by the seriousness with which it was covered by the national media.

1

Yet few believed that Jesse Jackson, or any black person, had a chance to become president in 1984.

effort he gained more support than any previous black candidate for president had received.

The responses to Jackson's candidacy by Democratic party leaders and the other Democratic aspirants confirmed the seriousness of his bid. He was given representation on the party's major convention committees. His objections to party procedures received the same kind of consideration as the objections of the other candidates. His name was included in national Democratic party mailings and fund-raisers. He appeared regularly in Democratic party presidential debates. In these ways, Jackson acted like, and was treated like, just one among the eight men who sought the Democratic party nomination in 1984.

The seriousness of his bid for the nomination was also confirmed by the response of the national media to his candidacy. National magazines put him on their covers both before and after he announced his intention to seek the party's nomination. All three television networks ran news stories that included in-depth analyses of and background research on the prospects of a Jackson candidacy. Leading metropolitan newspapers assigned correspondents to his campaign and followed it as closely as they followed the campaigns of the other major candidates. Television news stories consistently treated his campaign as one of many strands in the democratic process at work during presidential elections.

Yet few believed that Jesse Jackson, or any black person, had a chance to become president in 1984 (Cavanagh and Foster, 1984:2). It was assumed that the American electorate would not vote for a black candidate in sufficient numbers either to nominate or to elect him or her. To be sure, blacks had been elected mayors of several large cities in 1982 and 1983—but those cities all had large black populations. In congressional districts where black voters were a minority and in several highly visible statewide contests, blacks had recently run and been defeated. (Black candidates had lost to whites in congressional races in Mississippi and North Carolina, and Tom Bradley had lost the governorship of California in a very close race.)

Skepticism about Jackson's candidacy was not limited to the press or to party leaders. Some black leaders themselves did much to reinforce the notion that Jackson could not win and therefore should not run (Wilkins, 1985). For more than a year, black leaders debated whether Jesse Jackson or any other black person should seek the presidency in 1984. Black mayors and national civil rights leaders held several meetings on the subject but failed to achieve a consensus, and the most outspoken leaders explicitly opposed a Jackson bid for the presidency. (For an illuminating discussion of the black community's division over Jackson's candidacy, see Reed, 1986.)

The widespread perception that Jackson did not have a chance to become president[1] meant that although the media treated his candidacy seriously and with respect, they also gave it a different kind of coverage from the kind they gave other candidates. It has often been noted that presidential campaigns are reported much like competitive contests—and, in particular, like horse races—rather than as procedures for discovering and testing the candidates' capacities for leadership (see Patterson, 1980). To the media, the most important story in the campaign for a party's presidential nomination is who is winning and who is losing. The effect of this emphasis is that when a candidate is thought to be outside the circle of possible winners—when the candidate's victories and losses in the primaries seem equally irrelevant to the final outcome of the race for the nomination—the media treat that person's campaign differently from the way they treat the other candidates' campaigns. Presidential candidates who cannot win the presidency are like horses that cannot win a horse race. They are not newsworthy—or, at best, their story is a different one from the main racing feature of the day.

One way of demonstrating the effect of the "horse-race" emphasis is first to classify a large number of television news stories about the candidates in terms of the roles or role sets in which the stories present the candidates and then to compare the roles in which Jackson was cast with the roles in which the other leading Democratic candidates were cast.

In the context of a presidential campaign, "role" is defined as an expectation about how a candidate will behave when campaigning for the presidency. Someone—a candidate, a member of the public, a reporter—ex-

The widespread perception that Jackson did not have a chance to become president meant that although the media treated his candidacy seriously and with respect, they also gave it a different kind of coverage from the kind they gave other candidates.

3

pects a certain type of campaign behavior from a certain candidate. When that someone is a reporter, the expectation probably leads him or her to show the candidate in a role that reinforces and validates the expectation.

Research has shown that there is a symbiotic relationship between journalists' presentations of news and the public's expectations (see Arterton, 1978, 1984; Rivers, 1982). Thus, the roles in which television presents candidates affect the expectations of the members of the public who watch the programs. Reporters' preconceived categories of electoral politics, as expressed in the roles in which the reporters cast candidates, are transformed into the public's perception of the campaign.[2]

In the 1984 campaign for the Democratic presidential nomination, four roles, or role sets, were especially significant to television coverage. (Obviously, this list does not exhaust the possible roles.) The first set is Horse-Race Roles: reflecting the competitive aspect of the campaign, they have to do with the "current events" of seeking the nomination. The other three sets are Democracy Roles, Personality Roles, and Outsider Roles. Although not directly related to the winning of delegate votes, they may have a very large impact on a candidate's electoral success (as they did in Jackson's case).

Horse-Race Roles are of three types, according to whether they occur before the race, during it, or after it. Before the race, journalists are placing their bets about who will win, branding each horse with language that tells the betting odds for both the trial heat (i.e., the primaries and caucuses) and the feature race (i.e., the nominating convention). During the race, journalists are analyzing the strategy and tactics of each entrant. After the race, correspondents report who the winner is and who the loser is. This set of roles has evolved from political science and communications research on the influence of the mass media on elections and voting behavior.

Presidential campaigns are reported much like competitive contests—and, in particular, like horse races.

In **Democracy Roles,** candidates are shown fulfilling some of the responsibilities of political leaders in a democracy—that is, they are shown playing by the rules of the democratic electoral game. They court or represent various groups of citizens, criticize the opposition party, advocate positions on issues, and draw previously disaffected groups of voters into the electoral process. These

4

roles are based on several models of the way elections are supposed to work in a democracy.

In **Personality Roles,** candidates are the focus of background reports on their personalities, experiences, and attributes of character. The basis of these roles is popular and scholarly research on psychobiography and political socialization.

Finally, in **Outsider Roles,** candidates are shown (if applicable) as deviating from the accepted norms of political behavior. These roles represent the application of the political science research on outsiders in the legislative branch of government to the analysis of outsiders in the executive branch. (This "cross-disciplinary" approach was prompted by the question of a college freshman, who asked why political scientists don't use similar methods for studying the different branches of government.)

To learn how television treated Jesse Jackson in relation to other Democratic candidates for the nomination—in other words, to compare the roles he was given with the roles they were given—I analyzed the videotapes of 2,189 television news stories about one or more of the five principal candidates for the 1984 Democratic presidential nomination: Alan Cranston, John Glenn, Gary Hart, Jesse Jackson, and Walter Mondale. The stories appeared on the evening news programs of the three national networks between November 1, 1983 (the day candidates began announcing their intention of seeking the nomination), and July 19, 1984 (the day Walter Mondale received the nomination). Representing 47 hours of coverage, the videotapes (25 in all) were made available by the Vanderbilt Television News Archive of the Vanderbilt University Library.

I broke each news story into paragraphs and analyzed each paragraph for its dominant theme. I then coded the first four dominant themes in each story according to 113 categories that were relevant to my analysis. The categories were derived from the theory and research underlying each of the four roles. For example, the group of categories under Democracy Roles included a subgroup of categories that recorded whether or not a candidate was portrayed as a "spokesman" for some particular group, whether a candidate was described as popular (or unpopular) with some particular group, and

Presidential candidates who cannot win the presidency are like horses that cannot win a horse race. . . . At best, their story is a different one from the main racing feature of the day.

5

The roles in which television presents candidates affect the expectations of the members of the public who watch the programs.

whether polls showed a candidate gaining (or losing) the support of some particular group. This subset of categories pertains to the particular Democracy Role I call the Pluralism Role, and it is derived from the scholarly research on group theory and pluralism as a model of democracy in the United States.

Other information about the stories (date, network, correspondent, length, and so forth) and information about the campaign itself helped me make comparisons among the presentations of the various themes.

The group of Democrats under study was racially diverse and represented a fairly broad range of ideologies and chances of winning the nomination. Racially, one of the five Democrats was black and four were white. Ideologically, the five went from John Glenn on the right to Alan Cranston and Jesse Jackson on the left. In their chances of winning, one of the five seemed to me most likely to receive the nomination (he did in fact receive it), two seemed to me to have reasonable chances of winning the nomination (they did not), and two seemed unlikely to win it (and they did not). That broad variation makes it possible to compare both the candidates and the four sets of roles in several ways.

The Arrangement of This Volume

Chapters 2–5, which discuss one role apiece, contain two kinds of material. The first is a description of the role under discussion (and an account of the role's conceptual and historical underpinnings). This material provides a tool that analysts can use in studying television news coverage of any presidential nominating or general campaign. The second kind of material in Chapters 2–5 is the application of the tool to a collection of data from the 1984 campaign for the Democratic nomination, with particular attention to Jesse Jackson's candidacy. The two kinds of material—the description of the tool and the application—reinforce each other but can also stand alone.

Chapter 6 sums up the findings of the preceding four chapters as they pertain to Jackson's candidacy. Chapter 7 is an epilogue in which the analysis of the past is used to assess the future.

Endnotes

1. For a discussion of how the media affected perceptions of Jackson's chance of winning, see Gandy and Coleman, 1986. The authors measured the perceptions of college students after the students had been exposed to newspaper stories about Jackson.

2. Of course, candidates may or may not actually conform to the roles in which the media present them. And candidates may or may not perform campaign rituals expressly to evoke certain kinds of media coverage. But neither the relationship between a reporter's expectations and the candidate's actual campaign behavior nor the performance of campaign rituals for the particular benefit of television is the subject of this analysis. (For a discussion of how reporters' expectations influence candidates and the reporting of the campaign, see Greenfield, 1982.)

2. HORSE-RACE ROLES

The horse race has long been a popular metaphor for presidential campaigns. The press used the term "dark horse," for example, to describe Warren Harding when he became the surprise nominee of the Republicans in 1920. Since then, the phrases "dark horse," "front runner," "running neck and neck," and "it's a real horse race" have become part of the quadrennial electoral lexicon.

In analyzing television coverage of presidential elections, it is useful not to think of the horse race as a single event but to break it down into three different stages: before the race, during the race, and after the race.

Before the race, reports about candidates concentrate on the betting odds, or the chances that a particular candidate will win. The phrases referred to above emerge from this aspect of the race. A "dark horse" is a candidate who is thought to have only a small chance of winning the race. The "front runner" is the betting favorite to win.

The terms are mooted by the outcome of the racing event itself. **During the race,** voters, journalists, and political analysts take note of the tactics and strategy of each race horse. This particular focus became popular with the publication of Theodore White's best-selling book *The Making of the President 1960,* which he followed up with books about the 1964, 1968, and 1972 elections. Although White did not use the horse race to organize his own narrative, he popularized a style of campaign reporting that focuses on each candidate's campaign techniques and organizational strategy. White went back into the stables to see how the trainer, the jockey, and the owner spent their time and money in planning the events of the race. The result was a series of highly interesting and exciting accounts of presidential elections that have shaped election journalism for the past 25 years.

After the race, the main news reports describe who won and who lost. The horse race metaphor is helpful here, too. The big money winner (the recipient of a great

Before the race, reports about candidates concentrate on the betting odds, or the chances that a particular candidate will win.

9

deal of favorable publicity) may not necessarily be the horse that came in first; and if a front runner came in second or third, he or she may receive a disproportionately small share of the victory purse. Nevertheless, ending up "in the money" after a long series of state races is sure to have a high payoff in national party politics.

During the race, voters, journalists, and political analysts take note of the tactics and strategy of each race horse.

Before and During the Race

When describing campaigns as horse races, news reports often fuse two separate aspects of presidential elections: the state contests and the nominating convention. A television report, for example, may begin with the words "Front runner Walter Mondale campaigned in New Hampshire today . . ."—leaving it unclear whether Mondale is ahead in the overall nomination effort or in his popularity rating within the state of New Hampshire. Many references to a candidate's campaign activities *before the race* and *during the race* blend these contests. (Consequently, I coded both aspects of the campaign as Horse-Race Roles before the race.)[1]

Although all candidates would prefer to be ahead rather than behind in their quest for the nomination, the worst situation for a candidate is for his or her quest not to be discussed by television news at all. The importance of television news in presidential elections is so great that, in the words of one gubernatorial candidate, "If you're not on television, you don't exist" (quoted in Salmore and Salmore, 1985: 145).

A candidate who does "exist" in the horse race is assigned by television news to one of several positions: he or she will be considered—

- a front runner or likely nominee;
- a contender (that is, someone who "has a chance" for the nomination—and the chance may be "improving" or "fading"); or
- a dark horse or long shot (someone thought to have some chance, but a very slim one).

Assessing candidates in terms of their chances of winning a state contest can have the net effect of helping candidates who are behind and hurting candidates who are ahead. To be seen in the role of front runner early in the campaign (immediately before or after the New Hampshire primary), for example, can actually hurt a candidate's chances for upcoming state contests and ultimately for the nomination. Michael Robinson and others (1980) have pointed to what they call the "front-runner double standard." Front runners are often evaluated as political leaders who must prove themselves capable of winning whenever challenged, whereas other candidates are often evaluated only as campaigners who are working hard to catch up. In addition, the front runner is often singled out for criticism by several of the other candidates. In 1984, at least seven Democratic candidates accused Walter Mondale of being "too close to labor"—an accusation that hurt him in several early primaries and provided the Republicans with ammunition in the general election. Furthermore, when candidates are described as neck and neck with each other, it is the front runner—who had hoped to be perceived by party leaders as the most popular candidate and the one most likely to win the nomination—who appears at a disadvantage.

In this context, it is important to note the effect of polling on front runners. Most statewide surveys have at least a 3–5 percent sampling error; that is, the actual level of public support can be known with a high degree of confidence only within 3 or 5 percent of the poll results (for example, poll results of 50 percent support may mean in reality as little as 45–47 percent support or as much as 53–55 percent support). So a candidate needs to have support among at least 53–55 percent of the respondents in the sample survey before he or she can be declared the "probable winner" of a two-person contest. And when the percentage of undecided voters is high—as it typically is before presidential primaries—candidates are even less likely than at other times to have 53–55 percent support. Thus, the "front runner" going into the pre-election poll may often find himself or herself described as "neck and neck" or in a race that is "too close to call"—a report that makes the second-place candidate appear

After the race, the main news reports describe who won and who lost. . . . The big money winner . . . may not necessarily be the horse that came in first.

11

to be gaining popularity and the front runner losing popularity.

Furthermore, since most news reports concentrate on information about a candidate's viability (in contrast to information about a candidate's position on the issues, for example—see Chapter 3), "rational" voters who wish to reduce their expenditures of time and money in gathering information will support candidates on the basis of the candidates' probability of success—or at least will support only candidates above some threshold of probable success. This selectivity on the part of voters increases even further the viability of any candidate who appears to have a chance of winning in the polls—and that is good news for the second-place candidate who is declared to be in a race "too close to call."

The 1984 Campaign for the Nomination

In 1984, each candidate had *some* stories indicating he was in the race. Examples of the Horse-Race Roles in which television presented the four losing Democratic candidates follow, in chronological order:

January 27, 1984; ABC saw Glenn in a Horse-Race Role:

> As television commercials have reminded us for years, when you're number two you "try harder." John Glenn is running second in the polls to Walter Mondale, and that has prompted changes in Glenn's campaign.

The worst situation for a candidate is for his or her quest not to be discussed by television news at all.

February 20, 1984; on the day of the Iowa caucuses, ABC saw Cranston, Glenn, Jackson, Mondale, and others in relative standings that were based on their estimated strength:

> In an attempt to explain [the Iowa caucuses], let's take the imaginary town of Citizenville. . . . Let's say that 30 people go to the Mondale group, 20 to Glenn's. Fifteen people say they prefer Alan Cranston. Another 15 say they are uncommitted. The remaining 20 scatter in even smaller groups representing other candidates [video shows cartoon of citizens standing in front of Jackson, Hollings, McGovern, Hart, and Askew signs].

12

February 28, 1984; CBS, in Bill Moyers's live commentary on the night of the New Hampshire primary, saw Hart in a Horse-Race Role that demonstrates how reporters combine thoughts about state contests and thoughts about the nomination:

> Well, imagine what we would be saying tonight if it had gone the other way—if, on the basis of early returns and projections, Mondale had won a victory going away. Everybody would be saying, "All the Democrats have decided. It's over."
>
> It isn't over now. The polls aren't closed yet, but all the indications are we've got a two-way race here.
>
> The Hart people . . .

A look at the percentage of Horse-Race Role stories that portrayed one or another of the five leading candidates as a *contender* is instructive (see Figure 1). Cranston, Glenn, and Hart were described as contenders in approximately 33, 50, and 43 percent, respectively, of their Horse-Race Roles before the race. In other words, television news stories anointed each of those ultimate losers with contender status in about one third to one half of his stories. (Mondale was cast as a contender only 15 percent of the time, but that was because most of the stories assessing his chances for the nomination viewed him not as a *contender* but as a *front runner* or *probable nominee*.) Jackson, however, who was portrayed as a front runner in a few individual state contests, was portrayed as a contender in only 27 percent of his stories. In contrast, he was considered a "long-shot" candidate about as often, relatively speaking, as Cranston and more often than Glenn and Hart, the other two losing candidates. Hindsight shows that this measure of Jackson's standing relative to the other leading Democratic candidates was fairly accurate.

But this measure of Jackson's standing is a statement only about the distribution of his Horse-Race Roles. More telling is the number of times that television news placed him in any Horse-Race Role at all. As Figure 2 indicates, by this measure Jackson came in last among the five Democrats. In only 13 percent of all the Jackson roles did television news assess his chance of winning. The comparable figures for the other four candidates ranged from 27

[In terms of] the number of times that television news placed him in any Horse-Race Role at all, . . . Jackson came in last among the five Democrats.

Figure 1

Distribution of Horse-Race Roles, Before

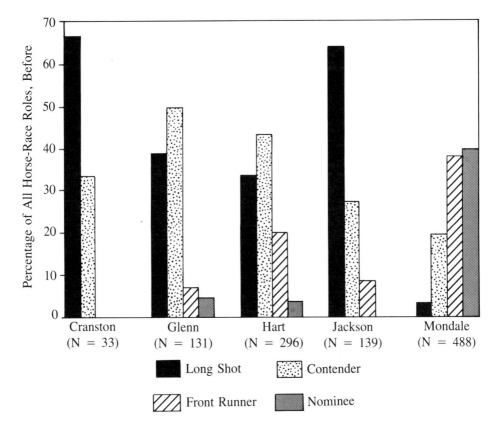

percent to 38 percent. It is not that television news was unfair in describing Jackson's chances; rather, television news simply did *not* describe his chances.

The difference between Jesse Jackson and the other four Democratic presidential candidates was reflected more in Horse-Race Roles during the race than in Horse-Race Roles before the race. Since reporters rarely assessed Jackson's chances of winning either a statewide contest or the nomination, they rarely referred to his strategy or tactics. In one of the few exceptions, on January 16, 1983, ABC

Figure 2

Horse-Race Roles, Before, as Percentage of All Roles

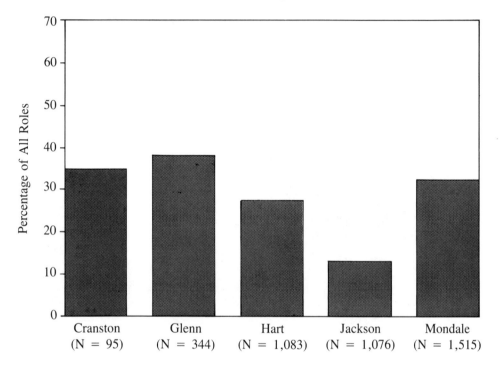

evaluated Jackson's use of televised debates for gaining voter attention:

> Jackson generated a lot of interest. Some of the other candidates were worried about his ability to debate even before they all sat down together. The viewers in New Hampshire who were polled thought Walter Mondale made the best impression. They judged Jackson to be the second most effective. And John Glenn the third.

But this focus on Jackson's successful use of a technique for influencing or impressing voters was atypical of most of the campaign stories about him in 1984. Other candidates were reported in relation to televised debates, factory visits, advertising, direct mail, and so forth. Jackson's use of those same techniques for gaining support was generally not looked on as newsworthy. As Figure 3 suggests, in

Figure 3

Horse-Race Roles, During, as Percentage of All Roles

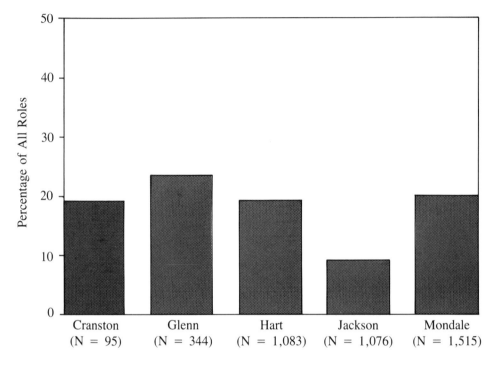

relative terms Jackson had significantly fewer stories about his campaign tactics than did any of the other four Democratic hopefuls.

The reluctance of television news reporters to assign a Horse-Race Role to Jackson before and during the race did not help his campaign. Contrast that with what happened in 1980, with John Anderson's campaign. Reporters described Anderson as a long-shot candidate and a dark horse, and even so, they continually praised his straightforward campaign style, his articulate presentation of the issues, and his experienced leadership qualities. Michael Robinson and others (1980) and Jeff Greenfield (1982) have both argued that this favorable television coverage persuaded Anderson to campaign even more vigorously for the Republican nomination and eventually, as an independent, for the presidency.

It is interesting to speculate about what might have happened if Jesse Jackson had received the same type of campaign coverage in 1984 that John Anderson received in 1980. After all, Jackson, too, could have been considered a long shot or a contender who had most of Anderson's attributes. Would Jackson have become a more important factor at the party convention? Could he have had a greater impact on the party platform? Would he have been considered for the vice presidency? Would he have been encouraged to challenge both parties as an independent?

While this exercise in "what if" is stimulating for historians and computer programmers, the fact remains that reporters did not look on Jackson as a possible nominee and therefore rarely cast him in a Horse-Race Role before or during the race. Almost no news stories spoke of him as the front runner (even though he won three primaries and caucuses), as a contender, or as a long shot. Few spoke of his campaign plans, techniques, and tactics. It is not that television news was opposed to his becoming president, any more than it was opposed to any of the other candidates. Rather, it simply could not imagine his becoming president.

After the Race

Horse-Race Roles after the race show candidates as winners or losers in state primary contests (caucuses, conventions, and primary elections) and reflect television's commitment to following the campaign as a sporting event. The horse-race metaphor requires that every state contest have at least one winner and/or loser—a journalistic brand that no state contest can escape. But Winner and Loser Roles are not assigned solely on the basis of an arithmetic calculation of the size of the purse (that is, the delegate count or the number of votes received). Other considerations are involved as well, complicating the meaning of Winner and Loser in television's terms.

It is not that television news was unfair in describing Jackson's chances; rather, television news simply did not describe his chances.

To television, not all primaries are alike. In addition to the number of votes received by all the contestants in a state race, the other factors that the media consider include the following:

- the number and political stature of the candidates who are entered,
- the timing of the contest,
- the nature of the governing state laws, and
- the procedures for aggregating results.

When two or more possible nominees actively campaign in a state, the media follow the campaign closely. For example, the Wisconsin, Oregon, and California primaries used to receive major television coverage because they were the proving ground for every possible presidential nominee. Now, because not all candidates always run in those relatively late primaries, major news coverage is given only if the front runner and one or two other possible nominees campaign there. In contrast, Florida was once looked on by candidates (and therefore the media) as an insignificant primary but now receives considerable media coverage because most of the candidates who are thought to have a chance of winning enter this early southern contest.

Like Florida, Iowa and New Hampshire draw much media attention because several possible nominees campaign there and because the caucuses (in Iowa) and the primary election (in New Hampshire) come early. The importance of early primaries will probably be accentuated in 1988, when many southern states will all hold their primaries on a single day early in the campaign. That so-called regional primary will increase the media coverage—and therefore the significance—of the primaries in the participating states.

Primaries in New York and Illinois are less significant than one might expect, given the importance of those two states at a nominating convention, because the procedures by which the voters show candidate preferences are complicated. Voters vote for delegates to the party's nominating convention rather than for presidential candidates. Moreover, it may not always be clear where the delegates' loyalties lie. And in Maine, which (like Iowa) holds cau-

The difference between Jesse Jackson and the other four [Democrats] was reflected more in Horse-Race Roles during the race than in Horse-Race Roles before the race.

cuses very early in the campaign, there is no central clearing-house for reporting the results; tallying up who won what caucus support can take two days. So by the time the results of the Maine caucuses are known, the news is already stale—leading television to ignore that early contest.

The variability of television coverage of state contests is reflected in the fact that Winners and Losers are declared only for some—not all—primaries, caucuses, and conventions, even though in every state contest one candidate necessarily comes out ahead. And not only does television sometimes fail to report the plurality winner, but it also sometimes fails to report the relative strength of candidates in those statewide contests where proportional representation is used to award delegates and where, as a result, relative standings are significant.

Primaries, caucuses, and conventions, therefore, are more than just contests for pledged delegates. They are also media events in which candidates may be featured in a Winning or a Losing Role. When a candidate not only gains the greatest number of votes in a state contest *but also* receives television coverage about the victory, he or she has won far more than a given number of delegates to the party's nominating convention. When television news presents a candidate as the victor in a state contest, voters in other states may well attribute a Winner Role to that candidate (Keeter and Zukin, 1983; Brady and Hagen, 1986)—and the converse is equally true. The cumulative effect of several such "television victories" in 1976, for example, raised Jimmy Carter from obscurity to the White House (Witcover, 1977).

In the states whose contests are treated as significant, the assignment of Winner and Loser Roles to candidates is made on the basis of—

- pre-election polls,
- exit polls, and
- a one-day (or longer) time lag between the closing of the polls and the media's attribution of Winner and Loser Roles.

Basing a Horse-Race Role on pre-election polls means that the vote a candidate receives is evaluated

In relative terms Jackson had significantly fewer stories about his campaign tactics than did any of the other four Democratic hopefuls.

in terms of the expectations that were held before the election. That is, the amount of support a candidate has (as measured by survey research) *before* a primary election becomes the key to descriptions of his or her status *after* the election. A candidate who beats the expectations is *for that reason* declared the Winner, even if some other candidate has actually received a greater number of votes.[2] Before 1976 that practice was common. After the 1968 and 1972 campaigns reporters were criticized for that kind of coverage, so in 1976 they focused on official winners of presidential primaries rather than on the candidates who beat reporters' expectations.[3]

The reluctance of television news reporters to assign a Horse-Race Role to Jackson before and during the race did not help his campaign.

A second basis for assigning Horse-Race Roles after the race is exit polling. Polls of voters as they leave the polling places allow the networks to discern trends before the 6 p.m. newscast and declare a Winner and/or a Loser on the day of the election. But that practice, too, has become increasingly controversial (see, for example, Milavsky et al., 1985). Critics of television news are concerned that the Winning or Losing Roles assigned to the candidates at 6 p.m. may encourage or discourage late voters from going to the polls at all. The data on this point are sparse, but Michael Delli Carpini's congressional testimony and research (1984) show that in areas where the evening newscaster has announced the results of a presidential contest before the polls have closed, voting in the local congressional contest has fallen off.

Trying to forestall legislation that would restrict their election coverage, the three major networks agreed in 1984 not to report exit poll results until the polls closed in the state being covered. Nevertheless, they violated the spirit of the agreement by characterizing the outcome of several 1984 primaries in general terms (although not reporting the actual tallies). And in states that are divided into two time zones (such as Indiana), or states where poll closings vary depending on locality (such as New Hampshire), they violated the letter of the agreement. Congress is currently considering several measures to curb the broadcasting of election results before all the polls in the continental United States close on election day. (For a summary of the pro-

posals and the research on this subject, see Tannenbaum and Kostrich, 1983; Sudman, 1986.)

Finally, the networks may allow at least one day
to elapse between the time an official winner of an
election or caucus is announced and the time they
make attributions of Winner or Loser Roles. The
lapse of time allows the networks to analyze the reactions of the candidates and the reports of print
journalists before making their political judgments.
Attributions of Winner and Loser Roles are, in fact,
more common the day after the official winner is
announced than the day of the announcement.

Some scholarly research on televised presidential
debates (research not directly related to primaries)
suggests that the importance of the media's attribution of a Winner or a Loser Role may grow as the
interval between the election and the attribution becomes longer. In 1976, for example, during one of
the televised presidential debates, Market Opinion
Research asked a sample of television viewers to report who they thought "did a better job—Gerald
Ford or Jimmy Carter?" The results showed that
Gerald Ford was thought to have won by 9 percentage points. Then reporters described several political
gaffes in Ford's responses to the panelists' questions
about Soviet influence in Eastern Europe; and in the
post-debate analysis on television, reporters suggested that Jimmy Carter's performance had been
better than Ford's. The morning newspapers
throughout the country carried a similar story. Poll
results on the day after the debate showed Carter
winning by 26 percentage points. After the evening
news on the day following the debate, Carter's lead
was 42 percentage points (see Steeper, 1978:85). A
similar process took place in 1984 with the first
televised Reagan-Mondale debate.

Thus, it may be that Horse-Race Roles after the
race are more important than the actual election returns. If in fact the television audience inflates the
significance of the election in the direction indicated
by the media's interpretation, then—at least until
the next race—the actual returns loom less large
than what the media make of the returns. Being
ahead at the finish by only 1 percentage point is one

*Primaries, caucuses,
and conventions . . .
are more than just
contests for pledged
delegates. They are
also media events in
which candidates may
be featured in a Win-
ning or a Losing Role.*

21

thing; but being ahead by only 1 percentage point *and* being called a Winner by the news reports is something else. Being called a Winner by the media may do a candidate more good—at least until the next race—than an actual victory does.

The cumulative effect of Horse-Race Roles after the race is to assign a negative or positive image to candidates during the preconvention period. Candidates who accumulate Loser Roles usually do not stay in the campaign for very long. Candidates who accumulate Winner Roles become possible nominees. Then there are the others—the candidates with few Horse-Race Roles after the race, the candidates who are generally called *neither* Winners *nor* Losers. By journalistic standards, those candidates are not considered possible nominees.

The 1984 Campaign for the Nomination

Such a candidate was Jesse Jackson in 1984. Television news generally presented him as neither a Winner nor a Loser in its coverage of the state primaries and caucuses. Even though he entered numerous state contests, adhered to and even challenged the rules of the selection process, and ended up receiving in statewide contests 12 percent of the delegates to the national convention, journalists rarely considered him for any kind of Horse-Race Role after the race, precisely because they never gave him a chance of becoming the party's nominee.

In those Horse-Race Roles it did attribute to him after the race, television showed no bias against Jackson in the valence of his roles (the ratio of Winner to Loser Roles). He was called a Winner in 44 percent of the Horse-Race Roles attributed to him and a Loser in 56 percent (see Figure 4). That percentage is considerably higher than the comparable percentages for Cranston and Glenn (both of whose campaigns were clearly less successful than Jackson's) and lower—but only a little—than the comparable percentages for Hart and Mondale (whose campaigns were clearly more successful). Cranston's 6 and Glenn's 37 Horse-Race Roles after the race were both distributed 1:9 between Winner and

*[I*n the relationship between Winner Roles and Loser Roles], television treated Jackson favorably.*

Figure 4

Distribution of Horse-Race Roles, After

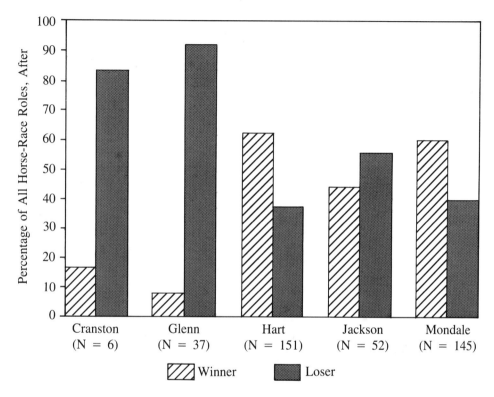

Loser. With his 4:5 ratio, therefore, Jackson looked much more like a Winner than did either of those other two unsuccessful candidates. Mondale's ratio was 6:4; Hart, ironically, received treatment equal to Mondale's, with 60 percent Winner Roles and 40 percent Loser Roles. Jackson's 4:5 ratio makes him look like almost as much of a Winner as Mondale, who actually got the nomination, and as Hart, who came close to getting it.

Of course, a candidate's percentage of Winner Roles should generally reflect the relative success of his or her campaign. And in these terms, by almost any criterion, television treated Jackson favorably. Jackson's 44 percent Winner Roles is higher than the 12.1 percent of delegates who supported him on the first ballot at the convention, higher than the 19.5 percent of votes he received in all the party primaries, and higher than the percentage of state contests (3 out of 52 [counting the District of Columbia and Puerto Rico], or 5.8 percent) in which he finished first.

But although the valence of Jackson's Horse-Race Roles after the race was relatively favorable in comparison with his actual strength and placed him in a category with Mondale and Hart, the volume of his Horse-Race Roles was not so favorable. Television news simply did not describe him as either a Winner or a Loser as often as it did the other candidates. Figure 5 displays the proportion of Horse-Race Roles after the race for each of the five candidates under discussion. Only 4.8 percent of Jackson's roles were Horse-Race Roles—descriptions of his success or failure in a state primary, caucus, or convention. That percentage is much smaller than the comparable percentages not only for Hart's and Mondale's more successful campaigns (13.9 and 9.6 percent, respectively) but also for Cranston's and Glenn's less successful and much shorter campaigns (6.3 and 10.8 percent, respectively).

Looking at the bases on which Winner and Loser attributions are made, we see that in 1984 the type of attribution that has more to do with the press's expectations than with a count of the votes actually cast was not very prevalent. In only 10 stories did the praise given to unexpected strength convert a losing effort into a perceived victory. Hart benefited from that exercise of editorial judgment in four stories, Jackson benefited in four, and Mondale benefited in two. The favorable publicity attendant upon those "surprisingly good showings," as they were often called, made a candidate who had lost in the voting booth look like a Winner on television.

Conversely, in three stories an official victory was turned into a perceived defeat. In one story Hart was declared a Loser although officially he won; in one story Jackson was; and in one story Mondale was. In such instances, television news either compared the outcome of a delegate selection

Television news simply did not describe [Jackson] as either a Winner or a Loser as often as it did the other candidates. . . . It was not that Jackson received unfavorable Horse-Race Roles [after the race]; he often received none at all.

Figure 5

Horse-Race Roles, After, as Percentage of All Roles

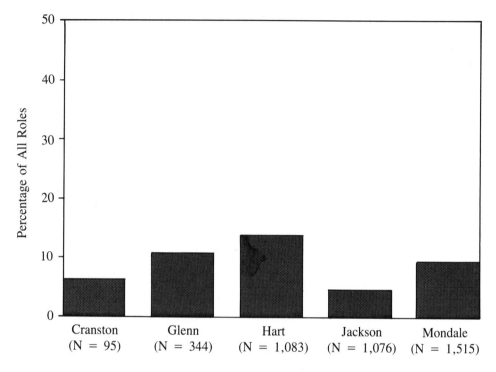

contest to the outcome of a previous electoral contest in the same state, or it measured a candidate's strength in a state against some unspecified higher expectation. Those two approaches are illustrated in the following stories. The first, about Hart, was broadcast on ABC on April 25, 1984, and the second, about Mondale, was broadcast on NBC on Super Tuesday (March 13, 1984).

Gary Hart won the Vermont caucuses yesterday, though not by the [amount of his] earlier win in the state's beauty contest. Then there were no delegates at stake and Hart won by 71 percent; yesterday Hart won by only 41 percent.

The Mondale campaign still is on hold. Mondale himself was publicly exuberant about winning in Alabama and Georgia, but his margin in Georgia was uncomfortably thin in a state that should have been a cake walk.

The second practice—the controversial one of calling election results on the basis of exit polls—was also used infrequently. The three networks used exit poll data to name Hart, Jackson, or Mondale Winners or Losers in only 29 stories (illustrating the maxim that a tentative news producer is safer than a tenuous news report) and gave Glenn and Cranston no such attributions. Moreover, the networks' sensitivity to calling election results with exit poll data led to many more attributions of Winner Roles than Loser Roles. Indeed, only 3 of the 29 attributions that were based on exit poll data declared that a candidate "lost" the election. It is perhaps noteworthy that all 3 of the "Loser" stories were about Jackson.

"Day-after" attributions were made in 255 news stories, divided almost evenly between attributions of Winner status (125 stories) and attributions of Loser status (130 stories).

The low volume of Horse-Race Roles after the race in television's coverage of Jesse Jackson confirms the finding that the coverage given to Jackson was different from the coverage given to the other Democratic party hopefuls. And the difference had significant ramifications. Regardless of how favorable or unfavorable the reports on Jackson might have been, because he was not granted "possible nominee" status in many of the races, his vote tally or exit poll results were often left out of the (graphic or verbal) presentation of statewide returns. It was not that Jackson received unfavorable Horse-Race Roles; he often received none at all. When he was a Winner in primaries and caucuses, television reported the story; but when he took second or third place in a statewide contest, he was generally not looked on as newsworthy.

Television's neglect of Jackson's standing in statewide contests had an important effect on the coverage given him as a whole. Since the most ex-

When he was a Winner in primaries and caucuses, television reported the story; but when he took second or third place in a statewide contest, he was generally not looked on as newsworthy.

citing aspect of campaign journalism is the assessment of who is winning and who is losing, candidates who run and lose are in a better position than candidates who simply do not qualify for the race at all. For even when television casts a candidate as a Loser, it generally allows him or her to "explain away" the defeat. And Jackson, like most other candidates, could generally find a nugget of hope in the worst defeat: he could point to overwhelming support from the black community or to the potential for support in an upcoming contest. Or he could use the occasion of a news interview to talk about the issues he felt were important. But when television ignores a candidate's standing in a primary, there is no interview or news conference.

Endnotes

1. News correspondents may not separate the two aspects in their own minds. From the media's perspective, each individual state contest (primary, caucus, or convention) becomes a trial heat, testing the candidates' popularity and campaign strategy with a sample electorate. Although political scientists and journalists often go to great lengths to demonstrate that no single state is, in fact, representative of the nation as a whole (for example, see Lengle, 1981; Polsby, 1983; Ranney, 1975, 1978), primaries and caucuses do test a candidate's general campaign strategy. Conversely, a nationally recognized party leader can reasonably be expected to show popularity and leadership among much smaller constituencies (such as the electorate within a state). Leading the country requires having the support of a large number of small, geographically circumscribed groups. For these reasons, the use of a single term to describe a candidate's chances both within a state and nationally seems appropriate.

2. Eugene McCarthy in 1968 and George McGovern in 1972, for example, were proclaimed "victors" in states where they received fewer votes than their opponents but more votes than pre-election polls had suggested was probable. Both inci-

27

dents affected their respective campaigns in important ways.

McCarthy's media "victory" encouraged Robert Kennedy to enter the Democratic campaign, and the two candidates waged a full-scale attack on President Lyndon Johnson's Vietnam War policy. McCarthy's "unexpected victory" in the early primaries and Kennedy's expected popularity in states with late primaries prompted Johnson to reconsider his decision to seek reelection; ultimately, on the eve of the Wisconsin primary, Johnson withdrew from the campaign.

In 1972, the media tagged Edmund Muskie as the "front runner" in the early stages of the campaign. His nationwide recognition as a popular northeastern U.S. Senator and as the 1968 Democratic vice-presidential nominee gave him an early advantage in the polls. The media referred to him as the probable winner of the New Hampshire primary by a large margin. But when he failed to win decisively in the Granite State, the media made much of George McGovern's "surprising strength" and gave him a media victory. That primary—and the way the results were reported—gave McGovern the recognition he needed to contest the Florida and Wisconsin primaries. He did, and he won both—catapulting to national prominence and, eventually, to the Democratic party's nomination.

3. Jimmy Carter benefited from the shift (Witcover, 1977). By entering all state contests he received television coverage every week regardless of the importance of the primary or caucus, and thus was cast in Winner Roles throughout February and March. That made him seem a successful long-distance runner. Unfortunately for more recent candidates, Carter's "marathon" strategy became the norm—for an exhaustingly long campaign.

3. DEMOCRACY ROLES

The person who emerges as president after a nominating campaign and a general election is the person chosen to act for the electorate on questions of public policy. Thus, for television to report on the "horse race," some media critics argue, is not enough. The daily or weekly excitement of the contest is eventually going to give way to the activities of governing the country. Therefore, television has the responsibility of conveying to its viewers what the candidates would be like—or suggesting what they might be like—as leaders of a democratic society.

Television fulfills that responsibility when it casts candidates in four Democracy Roles: Pluralism, Shadow President, Ideology, and Activator Roles. Each of the four derives from some model of how a democratic government ought to work, and together they help reinforce voters' beliefs that their own voices within the government will continue to be important and that the candidates for the nation's highest office are following the rules of the game.

Pluralism Roles

Pluralism Roles are the logical extension of a pluralist model of democratic government. The focus of that model is how citizens achieve political representation in a democracy. According to pluralists, the political representation of citizens is a function of group processes. That is, when people identify with, affiliate with, or join an organization (which is a group in institutionalized form), they are supposedly then able to speak in louder voices about society's problems and can exert greater influence on government officials. Conversely, government officials are held to be particularly sensitive to pressures from groups (or organizations). When groups have such politically valuable resources as a large membership, a substantial amount of wealth, strong lead-

Stories showing Jackson as a popular spokesman for large blocs within society helped legitimate his candidacy.

ership, or a compatible ideological position, politicians who need their support in the next election are held likely to give them favorable treatment.

Group theorists, whose concerns grew out of pluralism, posit three types of groups: primary, secondary, and tertiary. The essential differences among the three types are their proximity to the individual, their size, and their organizational structure. Those differences allow pluralists to provide an explanation for virtually all relationships between the individual and the government.

Primary groups are the groups with which a person comes in daily contact—the family, the school, and peers. Primary groups shape a person's fundamental attitudes and behavior patterns. From a political perspective, primary groups socialize children toward general and specific attitudes that subsequently affect their political behavior as adults. Of course, these same groups influence the political behavior of most "grown-ups," too.

Secondary groups are institutions, have formal structures, and owe their existence to a shared interest on the part of their members. People actually join, pay dues, and attend meetings to discuss a shared agenda that may affect their lives on a monthly or perhaps even a weekly or daily basis. Thus, secondary groups may claim to "represent" the interests of the entire membership. Churches, labor unions, civic organizations, and charitable organizations are examples of secondary groups. Some of them sometimes marshall their resources to effect political change, but many, or perhaps most, secondary groups make no attempt at all to exert political influence. Charitable organizations, for example, generally do not organize for the purpose of influencing government, and this is true even of charitable organizations whose boards may include politically influential people and whose activities may be largely dependent on government decisions. An example is the American Cancer Society, which is influenced by reports of the Surgeon General of the United States and receives grants from the National Institutes of Health, yet refrains from lobbying.

*B*ut Jackson's campaign suffered, as well, from his being cast in Pluralism Roles.

Tertiary groups are categories of people, rather than institutions; they do not have formal structures, and therefore their members have little or no formal contact with others in the group. They are generally quite large (larger, at least, than secondary groups). Examples of tertiary groups that have many members with well-articulated opinions on issues of public policy are blacks, Jews, and hunters.

The relationship between secondary and tertiary groups is not entirely clearcut, and pluralists' discussions of secondary and tertiary groups are often criticized. Secondary groups, which may claim to "represent" the interests of their entire membership, do not always represent the interests of the tertiary groups from which they draw their members. The NAACP no more represents the interests of all black people than the B'nai B'rith or the National Rifle Association (NRA) represent the interests of all Jews or all hunters, respectively. Nevertheless, the leadership of such secondary groups as the NAACP, B'nai B'rith, and NRA may claim to speak for the interests of their respective tertiary groups, and pluralists would see these spokespersons as representatives of the tertiary groups.

When pluralists turn from theory to practice, however, the relationship they posit between groups and the public's ability to be represented in government decision-making may break down. First, the model assumes that all people associate with some organization—but in fact not all people do join secondary groups. Second, the model assumes equal access by organizations to the structure of government—but in fact not all secondary groups have an equal opportunity to influence leaders. Third, the model assumes that organizations will form wherever there is a common interest—but in fact not all tertiary groups have secondary groups that can sustain a membership. (Two tertiary groups that were not represented in government decision-making until recently are welfare mothers and gays.)

*I*nvestigative reporters . . . found that the data did not substantiate [Jackson's] rhetoric and that his relationship to most of [the groups in the Rainbow Coalition] was not so very close.

This is not the place to discuss whether the pluralist model of government is appropriate for the American political process (see Dahl, 1961; Hunter, 1953; and Polsby, 1963), but in any case that model

31

has surely dominated American culture since James Madison wrote about it in the Federalist papers. In recent years, Philip Converse (1964) has observed that the single largest bloc of voters conceptualizes partisan politics as an expression of group interests. That is, voters believe their selection of government representatives is fundamentally a selection among competing factions within society.

Blacks themselves seemed divided about his candidacy. . . . That split . . . prompted numerous unflattering stories.

Not surprisingly, the model permeates the televised reporting of presidential campaigns. Television news often shows candidates relating to particular social and political groups, becoming spokespersons for those groups, and orienting their campaigns toward the groups—and when it does show candidates that way, it is casting them in Pluralism Roles.

A candidate's relationship to groups can be a source of both strength and weakness. On the one hand, appealing to *tertiary groups* is the most effective way to demonstrate the necessary popularity with large blocs of voters. Thus, candidates participate in the festivals and ceremonies of ethnic groups and partake of the groups' culinary specialties. In return, the candidates are portrayed by the media as participating in the rituals of American democratic elections, and their candidacies receive the mantle of legitimacy.

But on the other hand, a close relationship with the leaders of a *secondary group*, even one that can reliably claim to have a large membership, has political dangers. Candidates run the risk of becoming associated with so-called special interests whose lobbyists will supposedly extract political support later in exchange for campaign support now. The risk is particularly great when the secondary group is already unpopular with large segments of society.

The 1984 Campaign for the Nomination

The campaigns of the Democratic candidates in 1984 illustrate these contrasting aspects of Pluralism Roles.

Of the five Democratic candidates under study, only three—Hart, Jackson, and Mondale—were cast in a Pluralism Role to any significant extent. Relatively speaking, Jackson was portrayed in the role about as often as Mondale and a good bit more often than Hart (see Figure 6). Not surprisingly, the role Jackson was most often shown in was that of spokesman for blacks—that is, for a tertiary group.

The following NBC story of November 14, 1983, is typical. Indeed, it is typical not only of the way in which television cast Jackson in a Pluralism Role but also of the way in which group interests play a major role in American electoral politics. In fact, this story about Jackson could illustrate a discussion of pluralism in any textbook on American democracy.

Figure 6

Distribution of Democracy Roles

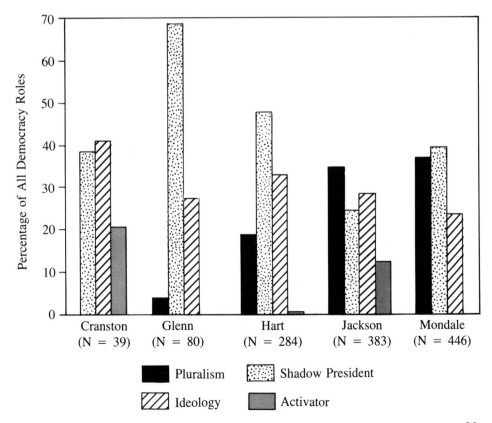

[*Voice*] The Reverend Jesse Jackson thinks of himself as the tip of an iceberg.

[*Jackson*] We're not just talking about one man running for office. We're talking about 10,000 running for 10,000 offices—and judge[s], and legislator[s]. . . .

[*Voice*] Jesse Jackson's campaign may be designed to move blacks into the political mainstream to join the Irish, the Italians, and others before them.

[*Jackson*] If you want a candidate who is blood of blood and flesh of flesh of the rejected, here am I. [*Cheers*]

Whereas Jackson's main Pluralism Role was as spokesman for a tertiary group, Mondale was shown mainly in relation to a secondary group—organized labor—that had articulated interests, was in the Democratic mainstream, and carried weight in the candidate's quest for the nomination. Ironically, however, Mondale's strength with organized labor early in the campaign became a liability later. In this instance, a candidate's ties to a secondary group were long-standing and the group seemed highly politicized in favor of that one particular candidate, allowing people to think that the candidate might be dependent upon the organization. This kind of symbiotic relationship has been considered particularly dangerous since Watergate, when close ties between special interests and candidates led to illegal campaign contributions and unsavory campaign activity. Although no one suspected clandestine operations in the 1984 campaign, the fact that the candidate was very closely associated with the special interests of a particular organization raised questions about his independence.

[A] set of Pluralism Roles that damaged the Jackson campaign consisted of stories about his relationship with Louis Farrakhan.

Of course, Mondale did court labor, especially in the early days of his campaign. The AFL-CIO held a special session at its annual convention to make its first pre-nominating-convention endorsement of a candidate. Television news covered the story, providing numerous shots of Mondale addressing the convention and shaking hands with leaders of organized labor.

Glenn and Hart charged that Mondale was "too close" to labor and had become a "tool" of labor's leadership. Television news covered those charges also, along with Mondale's countercharges. The ef-

34

fect of all the stories was probably to weaken Mondale's credibility as a broad-based candidate among Democrats and was certainly to give the GOP plenty of ammunition to use during the general election campaign.

Hart, like Jackson, was shown as appealing to a tertiary group, one newly identified in American politics: Yuppies. Those young urban professionals who had achieved positions of influence and standing in their communities by 1984 were the anti-Vietnam-War protesters of the late 1960s and early 1970s. Many remembered Gary Hart from the 1972 presidential campaign, when he was George McGovern's campaign manager, and many more approved of his upbeat and optimistic promises of a new leadership style.

The "Hymietown gaffe" . . . drew a great deal of attention to Jackson's attitude toward, and support from, the Jewish community.

Thus, although the coverage given to the Pluralism Roles of the three candidates was about equal in quantity, in quality there were differences. Television showed Mondale in relation to a secondary group or special interest (organized labor), whereas it showed Jackson and Hart in relation to tertiary groups or groups of people who just happened to have a characteristic in common (blacks or other purported members of the Rainbow Coalition for Jackson, Yuppies for Hart). Support from secondary groups goes against the post-Watergate ethic according to which politicians should not be dependent on campaign contributions that often carry a quid pro quo. Support from tertiary groups, in contrast, is consistent with virtually all campaign ethics, since by definition elections require the support of a large number of people. A news story reporting that large blocs of the electorate find a particular candidate attractive shows that the democratic processes of leadership selection are at work.

Because the specific groups supporting Hart and Jackson were not organized interest groups, as Mondale's labor support appeared to be, television news often created Hart's and Jackson's Pluralism Roles from opinion polls—a news event created by the networks—rather than relying on the events of the campaign itself. Furthermore, since neither Yuppies as such nor the groups that allegedly made up Jackson's Rainbow Coalition were organized, they could

Thus, . . . the Pluralism Roles in which Jackson was cast became the basis for largely negative publicity.

not be shown in the same way the national convention of the AFL-CIO could, with Mondale addressing it. So for Hart, the media occasionally showed young couples at a local discotheque or at a cocktail party in a fashionable home, where a banner proclaimed "Hart for President"; and for Jackson, the media talked about how the candidate was faring with the various nonblack groups in the Rainbow Coalition.

Consider the message to the television viewer who sees public opinion polls portraying one candidate's support whereas a film clip of campaign events portrays another's. For example, a CBS story on the day of the New York primary had a graphic display of Jackson's exit poll results, with the following voice overlay: "Jesse Jackson did extremely well with blacks, getting better than three-fourths of the black vote. But the rest of his Rainbow Coalition didn't show." Whatever the behavior of the Rainbow Coalition in the New York primary, the message to the viewer is that here is a candidate with the potential to win support from all facets of American society. Such images and reports, unlike a film clip of Mondale addressing labor's convention, used Pluralism Roles to create expectations about support from categories of people, not from politically active organizations. And support from categories of people, however weak it is, can demonstrate the genuineness of a candidate's appeal to some (albeit not all) citizens, whereas support from organized groups can appear inauthentic, contrived and staged. Thus, stories showing Jackson as a popular spokesman for large blocs within society helped legitimate his candidacy.

But Jackson's campaign suffered, as well, from his being cast in Pluralism Roles. Jackson himself claimed that his electoral strength would come from a "Rainbow Coalition" of groups disadvantaged both socially and economically (blacks, Hispanics, Jews, women, and the young). But investigative reporters, weighing Jackson's claim against media polls and election returns, found that the data did not substantiate his rhetoric and that his relationship to most of those various groups was not so very close.

In addition, blacks themselves seemed divided about his candidacy. Many black civil rights and religious leaders supported him with considerable reluctance, whereas most public opinion polls showed that young blacks endorsed a presidential campaign by a black candidate in general, and by Jesse Jackson in particular. Enthusiastic chants of "Run, Jesse, Run" in black church halls seemed to contrast with the reservations of the black leaders of the traditional civil rights organizations. That split in Jackson's natural constituency prompted numerous unflattering stories.

Another set of Pluralism Roles that damaged the Jackson campaign consisted of stories about his relationship with Louis Farrakhan, leader of the Black Muslims. Farrakhan is both popular and controversial within the black community, and television reporters were interested in showing how Jackson or other black leaders reacted to film clips of a Farrakhan speech.

Finally, what is known as the Hymietown gaffe (discussed in detail under Personality Roles in Chapter 4) drew a great deal of attention to Jackson's attitude toward, and support from, the Jewish community. After the "Hymietown" remark was made public, the attitudes of Jews toward Jackson were measured in public opinion polls and election returns, and Jackson's handling of the incident was generally reported in the context of Jewish support for him (or its lack).

Thus, although generally Pluralism Roles reinforce a candidate's campaign strategy, the Pluralism Roles in which Jackson was cast became the basis for largely negative publicity. He was indeed presented as a group spokesman, but it was as one who had divided support, was controversial and inconsistent, and may even have been dishonest with or antagonistic toward one of the groups he was claiming to represent. The combination of indecision on the part of black leaders, support from the controversial Louis Farrakhan, and Jackson's own "Hymietown" remark and unfortunate follow-up certainly destroyed whatever infinitesimal chance he might have had of being looked on as a possible nominee.

Yet, by scrutinizing Jackson's campaign in terms of its relationship to various groups, television news had a positive effect as well. It created a certain legitimacy for the candidate.

Yet, by scrutinizing Jackson's campaign in terms of its relationship to various groups, television news had a positive effect as well. It created a certain legitimacy for the candidate. Just as Mondale had labor support and Hart had Yuppie support, so, too, Jackson had black support. As a serious candidate for the presidency, Jackson received the same amount of media attention for his group support and opposition that any other serious candidate for the nomination received. That the media attention also hurt Jackson was, in the context of legitimating his candidacy, incidental.

Shadow President Roles

A second model of political behavior in a democracy is the responsible-party model, according to which an opposition political party exists partly to offer alternatives to the incumbent government (Ranney, 1954). A leader of the opposition is expected to criticize the incumbent party's management of government operations while supporting the structure of government itself. Television news stories reflect that model of democratic politics by casting candidates in Shadow President Roles.

Again, this is not the place to debate the merits of the particular model. Political scientists have already spilled much ink over the issue (see American Political Science Association, 1950; Turner, 1950; Ranney, 1954). In any case, reporters find this model of democracy particularly congenial because it fits their definition of news: competing factions that produce controversy, and identifiable people who will articulate opposing points of view. To a television news correspondent, any pair of interviews with members of the opposing political parties has the elements of a good story. There is an event (the interviews), there is controversy (the topic under discussion), and the controversy has balance (speakers from both the Democratic and Republican sides). Furthermore, because both the verbal and the visual forms of the story are usually predictable, news producers can use a set format when scheduling the story for news

As a liberal spokesman for the Democrats, Jackson was a relatively harsh critic of the GOP in 1984.

programs. Understandably, therefore, television news programs broadcast many campaign stories showing the candidates in Shadow President Roles.

In the United States, Shadow President Roles extend beyond inter-party competition. In a series of state primary elections, caucuses, and conventions, presidential candidates vie with members of their own party for the party's nomination. Those contests generate intra-party competition, to the extent that candidates of the same party often end up criticizing each other as much as they criticize the opposition party. Challengers within the incumbent party direct their criticism at the incumbent president; would-be nominees within the "out" party direct their criticism at the front runner of their own party; and a front runner often spends time answering critics within the party. Like rivalries between the parties, those within a party give rise to electoral debate and many opportunities for television to show candidates in Shadow President Roles.

Again [in the intra-party Shadow President Roles], because of his ideological position, Jackson received different television coverage from that given to three of the other four Democrats.

The 1984 Campaign for the Nomination

In 1984, television news cast the five Democratic candidates in inter-party Shadow President Roles in the following ways, according to whether the candidate or a surrogate was doing the criticizing and whether the president or the president's entourage and administration were the object of the criticism:

- A candidate was shown or described as criticizing the Republican president.
- A surrogate candidate (a friend or staff member) was shown or described as criticizing the Republican president. Candidates used this technique for criticism that was particularly harsh, so that they could make their point but not appear overly aggressive. In addition, Democrats wanted to avoid beating up on a very popular president.
- Either a candidate or a surrogate was shown or described as criticizing the Republican administration or one of its members (other than the president).
- A candidate was shown or described as making a broad, sweeping criticism of the Republican

party as a whole (for example, claiming that the Republican party favored the rich, but not specifying any particular program that produced that effect).

Of the five Democratic candidates, Cranston was cast in the inter-party Shadow President Role the highest percentage of the time; Jackson the second highest percentage; Hart the third; Mondale the fourth; and Glenn the fifth. (See Figure 7.) This rank order correlates highly with the left-right ideological dimension. Presumably the most conservative Democrat, John Glenn, found fewer points of confrontation with a conservative president than the

Figure 7

Distribution of Shadow President Roles

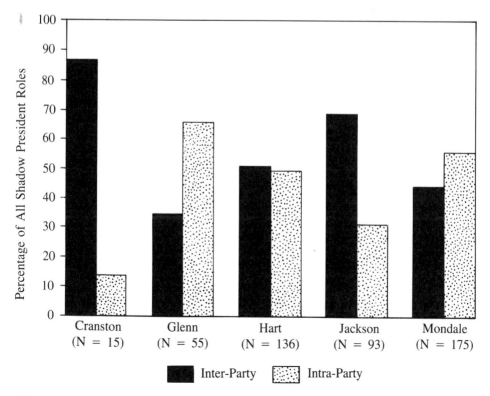

more liberal Democrats did. Similarly, the moderate Democrats, Hart and Mondale, were moderately critical of Ronald Reagan. As a liberal candidate, Jackson was surpassed only by competing liberal Cranston in attacks on the conservative Republicans. Thus, the presidency of Ronald Reagan stimulated partisan rhetoric more from the liberal wing of the Democratic party than from the conservative wing. As a liberal spokesman for the Democrats, Jackson was a relatively harsh critic of the GOP in 1984.

The pattern is reversed for the intra-party Shadow President Roles assigned to the five Democrats, as Figure 7 also indicates. The most conservative candidate, Glenn, was the one most likely to criticize a fellow Democrat. Moderate candidates Hart and Mondale were moderately critical; and liberals Cranston and Jackson were the least critical of the other Democratic candidates. Again, because of his ideological position, Jackson received different television coverage from that given to three of the other four Democrats.

The division of Shadow President Roles into inter-party and intra-party criticism, however, masks the major difference between the treatment given Jackson and that given the other Democrats. Ideology may help explain Jackson's tendency to criticize the opposition and refrain from criticizing his own party, but ideology does not explain the total percentage of Shadow President Roles that Jackson was given (Figure 6). No other candidate's Shadow President Roles constituted so small a percentage (24 percent) of his total number of Democracy Roles. Liberal Cranston (38 percent) and conservative Glenn (69 percent), as well as moderates Hart (48 percent) and Mondale (36 percent), had proportionally more Shadow President Roles than Jackson did.

Jackson, then, received different treatment when he criticized the incumbent president and other Democratic presidential candidates. In the Shadow President Roles that *were* given to him, the percentages of his inter-party and intra-party critiques were typical for his liberal position among Democrats. Yet as a whole (that is, in relation to all the Democracy Roles given him), he was seen as a critic (a

But ideology does not help explain the total percentage of Shadow President Roles that Jackson was given.

Shadow President) less than his fellow Democrats were. When television news actually covered Jackson pointing his finger, it covered the story as it did for any other Democratic hopeful; but apparently television news was simply not as interested in Jackson's finger as it was in the fingers of the other Democratic hopefuls.

Jackson, then, received different treatment when he criticized the incumbent president and other Democratic presidential candidates.

Ideology Roles

The two Democracy Roles presented thus far refer to what is expected of the candidates during a campaign—that they will connect themselves with tertiary and secondary groups and that they will criticize the other party (and perhaps the other candidates within their own party). The third Democracy Role adds a new dimension. Ideology Roles refer not only to what is expected of the candidates but also to what is expected of the mass media.

Ideology Roles are based on the direct-democracy model of government and, as the name suggests, this model stresses the importance of issues for the electorate's voting behavior. People who believe in the validity of the direct-democracy model hold that citizens express their preferences on public policy by selecting candidates who take the same positions on issues that they do. According to this model of democratic government, if the positions supported by the winning candidate were always enacted into law, the voters whose positions on issues most closely resembled the positions of the winning candidate would have a direct voice in government policy-making. The election of a candidate would become a mandate from the people for the positions that the candidate had advocated during the campaign—positions that were the basis for the candidate's having been selected by the voters.

Numerous books and articles dispute the empirical foundation of this model of democracy. For example, in 1954 Bernard Berelson and others depicted the public as issue-ignorant. Voters had apparently been unable to identify the position of an incumbent president on an issue, even though—

- the president had unambiguously fought for one side of the issue throughout his administration;
- the political parties had taken opposing positions on the issue; and
- newspapers had covered the issue as a front-page story for at least two years before the president's election to office.

These conclusions were replicated by Angus Campbell and others (1960) in numerous studies of the 1952 and 1956 presidential elections.

Concerned about the implications of an uninformed electorate, V. O. Key studied the rationality of voters in his posthumously published book, *The Responsible Electorate* (1966). He found a public that was more informed about issues of public policy than the public described in the previous studies. In the 20 years since publication of Key's book, political scientists have continued to argue these matters. (For a summary of the debate, see Niemi and Weisberg, 1976, 1984; Carmines and Stimson, 1980.)

Whatever position one takes, it is obvious that a precondition for an issue-aware electorate is media that are informative. Not only are the candidates expected to present their views on a variety of public issues, but the media are expected to report those views to the public. Without information about the candidates' stands on the issues, voters cannot base their election-day choices on the issues. It is precisely this educational function of the media that justifies the extra protection given to newspapers, magazines, radio, and television in the United States. Reciprocally, their special position obligates correspondents and producers of news programs to broadcast stories about the issue positions of the candidates—hence, the Ideology Roles in which candidates are presented on television. Television news, therefore, fulfills its obligation to serve the public interest when it casts candidates in Ideology Roles, showing them as advocates for positions on various issues. Similarly, most candidates seem to prefer being presented in stories on issues of public policy to being cast in Horse-Race Roles. Thus, the goals of both producers of television news and cam-

Ideology Roles were created in roughly equal proportions for all the Democratic candidates except Cranston.

43

paign managers are served by stories that cast candidates in Ideology Roles.

The 1984 Campaign for the Nomination

During the 1984 campaign, Ideology Roles were created in roughly equal proportions for all the Democratic candidates except Cranston (see Figure 6). Cranston was cast in the Ideology Role considerably more often, relatively speaking, than the others. This reflects the major characteristic of Cranston's campaign: with only one issue—a nuclear freeze—did he capture the imagination of potential supporters. He used that same issue as a basis from which to criticize the Reagan administration, receiving, as we have seen, a relatively high percentage of Shadow President Roles. That issue also gained him favorable publicity in a few early caucuses and party organizational meetings.

Cranston, then, had a disproportionately high percentage of Ideology Roles (41 percent). Among the other four candidates, Jackson was high at 32 percent and Glenn was low at 27 percent. Thus, there may have been a left-right differentiation in the coverage given to the candidates' positions on the issues, with the liberals (Cranston and Jackson) receiving more attention from television than the conservative (Glenn).

One explanation for the relatively greater prominence of liberal positions may be—as conservatives claim—that correspondents tend to be liberal and want to promote their own positions. (Social scientists have generally found evidence disproving that thesis [see Hofstetter, 1976].) A more reasonable explanation may be that the electorate's four-year drift toward the right had created a political climate in which the liberal positions of Jesse Jackson on civil rights and welfare and of Alan Cranston on a nuclear freeze made good news copy. Election news concentrates on differences between candidates, and reporters conformed to their own professional norms by juxtaposing liberal Democratic policies against the prevailing conservative policies.

In any case, it is easy to see why a candidate like Cranston had a relatively high proportion of both

A large number of Activator Roles . . . was assigned only to Jesse Jackson among the Democratic candidates.

Ideology Roles and Shadow President Roles. And it is easy to see why, given the groups Jackson was connected with in his Pluralism Roles, his proportion of Ideology Roles was slightly higher than the proportions of each of the remaining candidates. The several Democracy Roles tend to be as interconnected as the philosophical arguments from which they are derived.

Activator Roles

The fourth Democracy Role, the Activator Role, is derived from a participatory-democracy model of government, according to which the act of voting itself gives the public a sense of commitment to the structure and actions of government. This model holds that citizens are likely to grant legitimacy to the decisions of a ruling body when they participate in the processes by which leaders are selected. Researchers have found that many citizens feel a heightened sense of political efficacy after participating in the electoral process (Campbell et al., 1960): by helping to select the nation's leaders, citizens believe they are participating in the decision-making process.

Thus, according to this model, any candidate who encourages voters to go to the polls has, in a sense, helped continue democratic rule. Such a candidate is one who increases voter participation either directly (by conducting registration drives and get-out-the-vote campaigns) or indirectly (by heightening the interest of voters in his or her particular candidacy). The candidate who does either of those is a democratic Activator.

The 1984 Campaign for the Nomination

In 1984, a large number of Activator Roles (48) was assigned only to Jesse Jackson among the Democratic candidates. (The next highest number—8—went to Cranston.) Many reporters and Democratic party leaders, remembering how Eugene McCarthy's and Robert Kennedy's campaigns had appealed to the young in 1968, predicted that a Jackson candi-

Jackson certainly seemed to be drawing blacks—a group with historically low rates of registration and turnout—to the voter registration desks and voting booths.

dacy would increase the black community's interest in the campaign. They noted not only the success of voter registration drives in rural areas of the South but also the large voter turnout in many black precincts of metropolitan areas in the North and Midwest. Jackson certainly seemed to be drawing blacks—a group with historically low rates of registration and turnout—to the voter registration desks and voting booths.

The Democracy Roles in which television news cast Jackson both helped and hurt him.

But party leaders hoped for more; they hoped that increased black interest in the presidential race would help create a Democratic majority in the November election. To their disappointment, a disproportionately large black turnout did not materialize in November; of those blacks who did vote, however, 89 percent supported Mondale.

But even though the black turnout was not large enough to carry Mondale to victory in November (and, given the distribution of the white vote, could not possibly have been large enough), Jackson's role as Activator was still significant. He helped draw some blacks into the political process. He could claim success in connecting those previously disaffected members of a minority group with the electoral activities normal in a participatory democracy. Television news stories cast him in this role far more often than it did any other candidate.

Democracy Roles as a Whole

As a whole, the four Democracy Roles reflect what political scientists call the "rules of the game." That is, they reflect the written (constitutional and legal) and unwritten rules that determine how leaders are selected and how they derive their authority. As long as candidates are shown performing in Democracy Roles, both the candidates and the voters are reassured that citizen participation in the governing process is still taking place (Edelman, 1967).

For the candidates, Democracy Roles help legitimate their campaign efforts in their own eyes. The daily hoopla and public relations activities that the candidates must go through would seem like silly rituals if they could not be viewed as a manifestation of the rules of the game. Eating a pizza, kissing babies, and skiing in front of television cameras, however questionable their political relevance, have a significance beyond themselves: they allow candidates to establish rapport with diverse groups of citizens—from Italian Americans to working mothers to Vermonters, and others—and thus to demonstrate their loyalty to the democratic process.

Even more important, the assignment of Democracy Roles legitimates candidates in the eyes of the electorate. According to numerous studies, virtually all Americans give high levels of support to democratic norms in the abstract, and especially to the rules of the electoral game. Who in America, for example, disagrees with statements such as, "No matter what a person's political beliefs are, he or she is entitled to the same rights and protections as everyone else" (McClosky, 1964)? So when presidential candidates are cast in Democracy Roles, the electorate receives the implicit message that the candidates are abiding by democratic values in general and are conforming to the established rules and procedures of government in particular. The candidates are thus afforded a legitimacy without which even minimal success at the polls would be impossible.

The 1984 Campaign for the Nomination

In 1984, the Democracy Roles in which television news cast Jackson both helped him and hurt him. Most important, perhaps, television helped by legitimating him as a serious candidate. It presented him in basically the same Democracy Roles that it presented the other Democrats, and to roughly the same extent (see Figure 8). By doing so, television news took Jackson seriously as a candidate for public office. It implicitly acknowledged his standing as a full-fledged participant in the democratic electoral process.

However, the substantive implication of each Democracy Role is also important, and that is where there were real differences between television's

*M*ost important, perhaps, . . . television news took Jackson seriously as a candidate for public office. It implicitly acknowledged his standing as a full-fledged participant in the democratic electoral process.

Figure 8

Democracy Roles as Percentage of All Roles

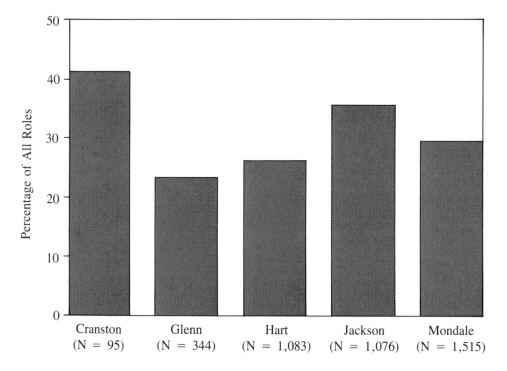

treatment of Jackson and its treatment of the other Democratic candidates. In the Pluralism Role, Jackson's candidacy was badly hurt; he was shown having problems with several constituent groups within the Democratic party. In the Shadow President Role, his criticism of the Republican incumbency and of his fellow Democrats received less coverage than one might have expected, given his liberal position. In the Activator Role, too, he was set apart, although it was for the creditable achievement of encouraging blacks to participate in the routines of politics. Only in the Ideology Role can we say that the coverage of Jackson in Democracy Roles was typical.

Thus, in Democracy Roles the way television news cast Jackson implied both that he was a legitimate candidate for the presidency and that he was somehow different from the other candidates who were also in the race.

4. PERSONALITY ROLES

When television focuses on a candidate's work habits, motivations for seeking the presidency, leadership abilities, and sense of humor, it casts him or her in a Personality Role. This is television at its best. In this kind of in-depth analysis of a candidate—the "backgrounder," as journalists call it—historical film clips may be interspersed with taped interviews and analyzed with video graphics. Despite the risk such reports run of seeming little more than "talking heads," they cater to the public's fascination with the rich and famous and are therefore particularly popular. As the networks have grown more concerned with ratings and corporate profits, the national news programs have increased the relative amount of time they devote to background reports (whether on political or on nonpolitical personalities).

When television news casts candidates in Personality Roles, however, it is doing more than providing entertainment. Indeed, from the point of view of a voter seeking to make a wise electoral decision, Personality Roles may be an especially appropriate focus for campaign news. Political issues, political parties, and the structure of government itself are likely to change in the course of a presidency, but personality is relatively fixed and may therefore be the best possible clue to the probable future behavior of a candidate. Voters might well be advised to choose candidates on the basis of a predictable factor like personality rather than a variable factor like issues and parties.

For example, comparatively sudden changes in issue, party position, and the structure of government came about in the aftermath of Watergate. Before the 1972 election, few Americans cared about the issue of campaign contributions, but the discovery that illegal contributions had been made to Richard Nixon's Committee to Reelect the President awakened the public to the dangers of unregulated political fund-raising. Also before 1972, the Republican party was opposed to the idea of allocating federal matching funds to presidential candidates—but in 1974 the party reversed itself and supported the measure as a post-Watergate election reform. Finally,

Proportionally, [television] reported vastly more stories about [Jackson's] Personality attributes than [it did] about [the attributes of the other hopefuls].

after 1972 even the structure of government changed, with the establishment in 1975 of a new regulatory agency, the Federal Election Commission. None of those changes—in issue, party position, or the structure of government—could have been anticipated during the election of 1972 by even the most informed voter.

When Horse-Race Roles are lacking, the personality or background of the candidate can substitute for the horse race as a context within which to report on the day's news.

Conversely, the usefulness of analyzing candidates in terms of their personality can also be shown by an example taken from Watergate. James David Barber's psychobiography of Richard Nixon (1972, 1977) would have been a more reliable guide to selecting a president in 1972 than a study of issues and parties or a reaction to Nixon's first administration. The book's first edition accurately predicted how Nixon would behave during a presidential confrontation with Congress, claiming that he would withdraw from public office and ultimately from public life if his authority were ever seriously challenged. Barber's training in analyzing presidential personality may not be part of every citizen's equipment, but every citizen can read or hear about personality traits, and in 1972 such traits constituted the best information available to voters who were reluctant to reelect Nixon but needed a basis on which to make their decision.

The 1984 Campaign for the Nomination

In casting the 1984 Democratic candidates in various Personality Roles, television clearly treated Jackson differently from the other hopefuls. Proportionally, it reported vastly more stories about his Personality attributes than about theirs (see Figure 9). Jackson was at least five times more likely than any other Democratic candidate to have his Personality or background discussed in a news story.

At least three things account for the attention given to Jackson's Personality. First, he is flamboyant. His language, delivery, and mere presence generated an enthusiasm in his audiences that was unmatched by the reactions any other candidate was able to arouse.

Second, journalists associated Jackson's rise to national prominence with a personality trait—the trait of opportunism. Jackson has a knack for being in the right place at the right time, and many jour-

Figure 9

Personality Roles as Percentage of All Roles

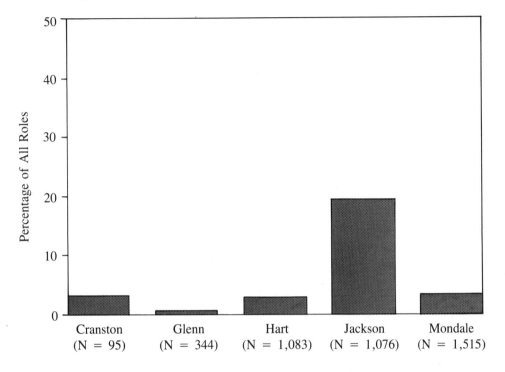

nalists believe that when he is not in the right place, he is capable of bending the truth to put himself there (Wilkins, 1985).

The publicity surrounding the death of Martin Luther King, Jr., illustrates the point. Few people would dispute that Jackson was a close associate of the late civil rights leader, and he was unquestionably present in the Memphis motel when King was shot. But eyewitnesses to the event say that Jackson was in his own first-floor room when King was shot on the balcony of a second-floor room. Nor was Jackson the first person to reach King after the murder. However, in Jackson's subsequent public recounting of the incident, he placed King in conversation with him, Jackson, at the time of the shooting. Thus, he claims to have heard Martin Luther King's last words, which allegedly were about civil rights strategy for the coming years.

For some, bending facts at a time of national mourning was irreverent at best and premeditated opportunism at worst. Jackson's version of the incident conveyed the message that he was the heir apparent to the throne left vacant by King's death. After all, both were preparing the next step in the civil rights movement at the moment the leader's life was ended. Who would be a better replacement for King than the leader's close confidant? To some, therefore, Jackson had manipulated the symbols of a tragically shocking event to his own political advantage.

Perhaps Jackson's detractors among the press saw a presidential bid as yet another example of Jackson's manipulation of symbols. If he had manipulated the publicity surrounding the death of a civil rights martyr, he surely would manipulate the symbols of presidential elections. Skeptical reporters told television viewers about this characteristic of Jackson's personality and style.

The third reason for the attention given to Jackson's personality, and the one most important for this analysis, has to do with the absence of Horse-Race Roles for Jackson. As has been discussed, the most important element in an election story is who is winning and why. Most campaign reports are placed within that context; the news events of the day are reported in terms of their effect on the candidate's probability of winning. The day's events provide the news, while the probability of winning is the story, or peg, to hang the news on.

Television's emphasis on Jackson's hard campaign work and on his prolonged negotiations with foreign officials were all the more welcome to the candidate . . . since, at first glance, people have the impression he is merely a show horse.

But when Horse-Race Roles are lacking, the personality or background of the candidate can substitute for the horse race as a context within which to report on the day's news. Like the horse race, personality is a long-term characteristic. The events of the day are one manifestation of a more general story to be reported, but in Jackson's case, since he was not a possible nominee, the larger story (the long-term context) was his personal characteristics.

Generally there are at least four Personality Roles into which candidates tend to be cast: the Worker, the Opportunist, the Entertainer, and the Role Model.

Worker and Opportunist Roles

The Worker Role is important in American politics, and being shown in a Worker Role reflects favorably on a candidate's ability to operate effectively in Washington. Some researchers who have analyzed how political power is gained and used in the Senate, for example, have shown that in that body, hard work is a prerequisite for achieving power. Donald R. Matthews (1960) notes that mere ''show horses'' do not often assume positions of leadership in the upper house. Instead, Senate newcomers must work at the laborious tasks of studying the rules of the Senate, learning the intricacies of specific pieces of legislation, attending committee meetings, and demonstrating impeccable manners to elder colleagues if they wish eventually to attain positions of influence and power.

With the presidency the situation is somewhat similar, although hard work on a daily basis is not a prerequisite for becoming either a successful or a popular president (Barber, 1977). Nevertheless, knowledge about the amount of work in a president's daily routine helps us understand his leadership style. Herbert Hoover, Franklin Roosevelt, and Richard Nixon were all ''active'' presidents who worked hard at the daily chores of their office. When confronted with crises such as the Great Depression, World War II, and Watergate, they all devoted huge blocks of time to the problem, albeit with varying degrees of success. In contrast, both Dwight Eisenhower (whom scholars now consider to have been a fairly successful president [see, for example, Greenstein, 1982]) and Ronald Reagan (who, until the selling of arms to Iran became public, was extremely popular) can be described as ''passive.'' Eisenhower even managed to play golf during the Suez crisis of 1956, and Reagan was not publicly upset when presidential advisor Edwin Meese allowed the president to sleep through the

By emphasizing the work-horse aspects of his character, . . . television news stories helped strengthen Jackson's presidential credentials.

2 a.m. dogfight between U.S. Navy fighters and Libyan fighters over the Gulf of Sidra in 1981. A candidate's propensity for or avoidance of hard work is therefore an appropriate subject for campaign news, since it helps us understand the leadership style that person will demonstrate during his or her term of office as president.

*B*ut . . . *one person's hard work may be another person's opportunism.*

A corollary to the Worker Role is the Opportunist Role. Did Lyndon Johnson's climb to political power, for example, result from his never-ending energy and hard work—or from his exploitation of weak leaders and ambiguous political situations? The answer to that question probably depends on whether one admires or abhors Johnson. In other words, a politician's hard work may, to his or her detractors, be exploitation and opportunism.

The 1984 Campaign for the Nomination

In the reports on Jackson's Personality, both his admirable and his not-so-admirable habits and qualities were discussed, and the quality that seemed most admirable was his stamina, his penchant for hard work. About 53 percent of the Personality stories about him dealt with his hard work, his incredible energy: the long hours he spent planning, organizing, and traveling with his campaign, the endless string of projects he set in motion to help South Side Chicago blacks, the lengthy meetings and arduous negotiations he held with foreign leaders during the campaign. This percentage is comparable to Hart's (54 percent) and larger than Mondale's (30 percent)—see Figure 10.

Television's emphasis on Jackson's hard campaign work and on his prolonged negotiations with foreign officials were all the more welcome to the candidate and his supporters since, at first glance, people have the impression he is merely a show horse—the kind of flashy political animal who, in the Senate, would rarely become a member of the inner circle. Jackson's manner is flamboyant and as a speaker he is funny, entertaining, and quick-witted. So by emphasizing the work-horse aspects of his character, television helped the public become aware of those less obvious but politically signifi-

Figure 10

Distribution of Personality Roles

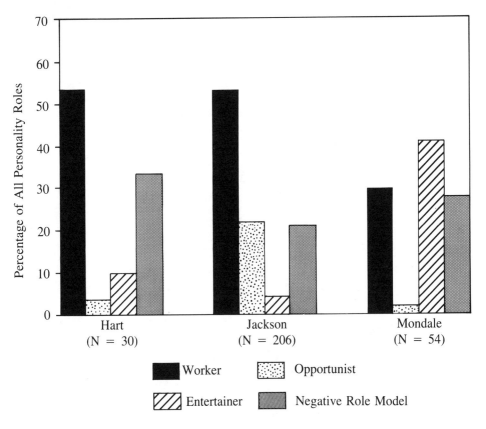

Worker ■   Opportunist ▦

Entertainer ▨   Negative Role Model ▨

cant qualities. In that respect, television news stories helped strengthen Jackson's presidential credentials.

But at the same time, as we have seen, one person's hard work may be another person's opportunism. On the one hand, television news stories appropriately gave prominence to Jackson's industriousness, which Roger Wilkins (1985), for example, argues is Jackson's most salient characteristic. But on the other hand, about 20 percent of all the stories that cast Jackson in a Personality Role discussed his foreign policy labors not as something praiseworthy but as a manifestation mainly of opportunism. Stories dealing with his trips to Syria, Cuba, and Central America all viewed those trips not as instances of hard work but as part of his campaign strategy. Obviously, Jackson timed his foreign travel to gain maximum publicity; but correspondents implied that he planned activities for their publicity value more than the other candidates did.

The news reports during the period that led up to the release by Syria of captured U.S. Navy pilot Lieutenant Robert Goodman are a good case study for an analysis of television's treatment of Jackson. With the obvious benefit of hindsight, we can see how correspondents' cynicism produced counter-factual analyses of the event. Dan Rather introduced a story about Jackson's trip to Syria this way:

> After voicing second thoughts about his trip to Syria, Democratic presidential candidate Jesse Jackson apparently had third thoughts and changed his mind. He's bound for Syria tonight on a self-appointed mission to try to gain the release of captured U.S. Navy flier Robert Goodman, Jr. Jackson calls it a "mission of hope"; some others are calling it "mission impossible"—even a "grand-standing ego trip."

Bob Fall's tag line to the story was as follows:

> What some regard as an election stunt is great at getting Jesse Jackson exposure. The question, of course, is whether it's any good at getting results—in this case, the release of Lieutenant Goodman.

Or the tag line on a CBS story from Damascus on December 30, 1983:

> Getting here got Jesse Jackson a lot of ink and air time, but now the burden has shifted to him to show that everything here that smacks of campaigns will help and not hinder getting Lieutenant Goodman out.

Goodman, as we know, was released. The accomplishment of "mission impossible" moots all discussion of Jackson's motivation. It simply does not matter why he went to Syria, given that in the end he was able to do what America's Chief Diplomat had been unable to do. (Now, three years later, we can appreciate the extent of Jackson's skill in obtaining Goodman's release: Jackson neither violated U.S. laws nor gave up millions of dollars' worth of arms to gain this hostage's freedom.)

About 20 percent of all the stories that cast Jackson in a Personality Role discussed his foreign policy labors . . . as a manifestation mainly of opportunism.

The pre-Syria stories emphasized Jackson's opportunism rather than his international symbolism as a black leader, his skills as a diplomat, or even his extensive preparation for the trip. After Goodman's release, the news reports were quite favorable to Jackson—presenting his accomplishment as a major diplomatic success. If he had not succeeded, however, we would probably have heard more about his "ego trip."

But the charge of opportunism may have had some foundation after all. First, unlike the other Democratic contenders, Jackson had little funding for paid television advertising and therefore had to rely on "free media" more than they did. News coverage was the only way he could get television to carry his message; and being "newsworthy" enough to keep the cameras rolling may have meant occasionally scheming and holding some inauthentic news conferences.

Opportunism, of course, may be another name not merely for hard work but also for leadership, and in this sense Jackson's bid for publicity was nothing out of the ordinary. He was not the first presidential aspirant to take advantage of free television publicity to achieve a position of national prominence. Estes Kefauver used his Senate hearings on organized crime to become the Democratic vice presidential nominee in 1952; Eugene McCarthy used his crusade against the Vietnam War in 1968 to drive the president of his own party into retirement; and George McGovern used his Senate hearings on hunger in America as a springboard to the Democratic presidential nomination in 1972. All three of them gained television news coverage that advanced their political aspirations, and all could have been labeled opportunists. Even Robert Kennedy, in his 1968 bid for the presidential nomination, and Hubert Humphrey, in taking the "high road" to the nomination in that same year, were charged with opportunism. Seen in this context, Jackson's tactics were a normal part of the game of electoral politics. By definition, a campaign is an effort to gain publicity with speeches and activities that will attract media attention, and Jackson was simply playing the usual game.

Wit is a second admirable quality that Jackson has in abundance, but . . . his wit was underplayed or not captured at all by television news.

On the whole, then, television took one of Jackson's most significant admirable qualities—his energy, or stamina—and made it known to the public. The context within which that quality was presented, however, turned it into a campaign handicap as well as an asset, since what a sympathetic observer sees as hard work can, to a detractor, look like opportunism.

[Thus,] he did not benefit from the good will that most people extend to a person with a lively sense of humor.

Entertainer Role

Some people bring wit and humor to even the most serious task. Certainly, running for president of the United States is no joke (although comedians such as Pat Paulson and Chevy Chase have built careers on satirizing presidential campaigns), but funny phrases and light-hearted comments can personalize and give a lift to speeches that would otherwise seem dull and uninspired. The Entertainer Role usually enhances a candidate's image.

Humor—like hard work—has a long and honorable tradition in American politics, and because of it the media may be likely to cast a candidate in the combined role of Entertainer-Master Politician. John F. Kennedy, for example, learned to use wit very effectively to deflect difficult questions at presidential news conferences. Lyndon Johnson, Hubert Humphrey, and Barry Goldwater all used humor in gaining the friendship and respect of their colleagues in the Senate (and all were masters at translating that personal respect into political influence). Ronald Reagan used humor to blunt concern about his age in the second televised presidential debate with Walter Mondale in 1984. Wit, in other words, can have consequences greater than merely the laughter it evokes.

The 1984 Campaign for the Nomination

Wit is a second admirable quality that Jackson has in abundance, but unlike his hard work, his wit was underplayed or not captured at all by television news (see Figure 10). In fact, television news presented more one-liners by Walter Mondale, perhaps the campaign's most boring personality, than by Jackson. Thus, because television news stories about Jackson's humor were relatively scarce, some of his charm was underplayed. He did not benefit from the good will that most people extend to a person with a lively sense of humor.

Role Model

In the final Personality Role, a candidate may be presented as a Role Model (whether positive or negative). According to the psychological theory underlying the concept of role model, a "significant other" is central to personality development: personality is held to develop from myriad dyadic relationships between an individual and the people who make up his or her immediate environment (mother, father, teacher, friend, and so forth). In the popularized version of that theory, a positive role model is someone special with whom a person, usually a child or adolescent, identifies and after whom the young person patterns his or her own life goals. A negative role model is someone special whose behavior is to be deplored rather than emulated. The concept of role model is particularly relevant in the context of presidential politics. Since presidents seem larger than life to most citizens, it is especially important for a presidential candidate to appear to be good "role model" material.

Numerous studies have shown that most citizens view presidents favorably rather than unfavorably. Most citizens have a positive image of whatever person is president, especially in the early days of a new administration (Mueller, 1973:196–231; Rubin, 1981:221). Although presidential popularity shrinks slightly in the course of a four-year term as the incumbent conducts the routine affairs of government, virtually all presidents retain a relatively high level of popularity throughout their administrations. Then, at the next election, citizens are encouraged to reevaluate their support of the president if the incumbent chooses to run for reelection.

The way in which Jackson was cast [as a Role Model] was very damaging to him.

61

The image of the president as benevolent is thought by some researchers to be particularly important in the political socialization of children. Even before children have the capacity to reason causally and to evaluate critically, they generally attribute positive characteristics to the president, and the researchers argue that a positive image of the president in early childhood forms the basis on which, as an adult, a person comes to accept political authority (see, for example, Easton and Dennis, 1969; Hess and Torney, 1967; and Greenstein, 1965). Thus, by fulfilling the function of a positive role model, each president helps to maintain the continuity of trust in government from one generation to the next. Nixon's false statements and vulgar and prejudiced expletives were especially damaging in this respect, since they undermined the image of benevolent government that is so important to children.[1]

Presidential candidates whom television news presents as having many positive personal attributes will seem particularly worthy of public trust. Presidential candidates shown with several negative personal attributes will seem unsuited for it.

To analyze candidates as Negative Role Models requires one to inspect the actual *number* of roles of this kind rather than the *percentage* of Personality Roles devoted to such incidents. This is because negative publicity in a campaign can be so damaging. A single political gaffe can cause a candidate to become a "scratch horse" very quickly. One such infamous blunder was George Romney's admission of having been "brainwashed" during his 1968 visit to Vietnam. Another was Edmund Muskie's tearfulness at a press conference in 1972, called to rebut the local newspaper's accusations about his wife. And, of course, Gary Hart's 1988 presidential bid came to a premature end with the publicity surrounding his weekend visit from an attractive blond model. For Romney, Muskie, and Hart, one Negative Role Model was enough to do severe damage to their respective campaigns—even if, in overall terms, the one incident was only a small percentage of the total number of stories about the candidate.

He engaged in some behavior and made some statements that could have been construed as those of a man who was neither decent nor honest.

The 1984 Campaign for the Nomination

The way in which Jackson was cast in this final Personality Role was very damaging to him. This role derived not from his daily habits and characteristics of personality but from some of his political behavior and campaign statements—and he engaged in some behavior and made some statements that could have been construed as those of a man who was neither decent nor honest. Television news made heavy use of his behavior and statements, handling them in such a way that he did indeed seem a Negative Role Model for decent, honest citizens. In fact, for Jackson as for Romney and Muskie before him, the combination of the candidate's own behavior and statements and television's reporting of them probably meant he was eliminated from consideration as a presidential candidate.

The combination of the candidate's own havior and statements and television's reporting of them probably meant he was eliminated from consideration as a presidential candidate.

The problem began with an ethnic slur, and it was compounded by Jackson's follow-up behavior. Ethnic slurs have long been taboo in national politics, and the civil rights movement made Americans particularly sensitive to the stereotyping of minorities. A candidate or office holder who refers to a racial or ethnic group in a derogatory way becomes a liability to himself or herself or to the person he or she is supporting. In 1968, vice presidential candidate Spiro Agnew was discredited when he called a reporter a "fat Jap"; Earl Butz had to resign from Gerald Ford's cabinet when he made a racist joke about blacks; and James Watt had to resign from Ronald Reagan's cabinet when he belittled several minority groups in one sentence.

In 1984, Jesse Jackson became the latest national political figure to learn that insensitivity to an ethnic group is bad politics. In private remarks, he referred to New York City as "Hymietown" and to Jews as "Hymies" (for a discussion of these remarks, see Faw and Skelton, 1986). When the remarks were made public by a reporter, they became a story with a devastating effect on Jackson's campaign. To understand why a defamatory comment about Jews by a black presidential candidate became an important campaign story, one needs to understand the context.

The [Hymietown] incident shed various negative lights on the candidate. . . . He offended Jews, . . . he offended civil libertarians, . . . he offended moralists, [he offended] Democrats in general.

First, American Jews are strategically important in presidential campaigns, partly because they contribute large sums of money and partly because they are concentrated in the largest industrial states. Thus, they have been courted by most Democratic presidential candidates and, recently, by Republicans with a pro-Israel policy position.

Second, in recent years the relationship between Jews and blacks has been less harmonious than it used to be. In the early 1960s, Jews and northern blacks cooperated to help register southern blacks at the polls. Two Jewish volunteers who were murdered in a small Mississippi town during those registration drives became a symbol of Jewish-black unity. But in subsequent years, the myth of Jews as slumlords and blacks as their exploited tenants considerably weakened the alliance of the two minority groups, both of which were considered essential for Democratic presidential victories.

The weakening of the alliance became especially evident in 1982 during the Chicago mayoralty race—a local campaign with considerable national implications. Democrat Harold Washington, a South Side Chicago black politician who had served in the U.S. House of Representatives, defeated Republican Bernard Epton, a Jewish businessman. That campaign received national attention because the Democratic primary had resulted in the defeat of an incumbent mayor—a startling outcome for a city where machine politics had dominated local elections through the mid-1970s. The general election between a black and a Jew symbolized the disintegration and the dis-integration of the Chicago Democratic party. In the following year another black, Wilson Goode, was elected mayor of Philadelphia—another city known for its Democratic coalition of ethnic groups. Although the voting data do not show as wide a division between blacks and Jews in Philadelphia as in Chicago, Jackson presumably felt he could ride the wave of black success that brought Washington and Goode to office, without being especially sensitive to groups (including Jews) that had abandoned the two black mayors.

Third, Jackson's peace mission to Syria in December 1983, like his continuing criticism of Israel's West Bank settlements, had already raised questions about his position on Israel, an issue important to American Jews. Although the trip resulted in the release of the captured American pilot (and brought Jackson favorable publicity, including a congratulatory meeting at the White House with Ronald Reagan), supporters of Israel were not pleased. Jackson's accomplishment seemed to have been facilitated by ties to militant Arabs at the same time that Israel was fighting a war in Lebanon against militant Arabs.

Moreover, supporters of Israel were also wary of Jackson for having embraced Yasser Arafat, the leader of the Palestine Liberation Organization. Pictures of the two men meeting in 1979 had appeared in the national media and created a perception that Jackson was friendly toward Israel's most determined enemy. Even before the Hymietown remark, Jewish leaders had used one of those photographs to try to discredit Jackson's campaign in the minds of Jews.

This was the context within which a defamatory comment by a black presidential candidate about Jews became an important political story. Jackson's remark seemed a political gaffe of the same kind as Richard Nixon's endorsement of ''benign neglect'' for the poor in 1970, Gerald Ford's reference to a ''free Poland'' in 1976, or Jimmy Carter's discussion of ''ethnic purity'' in 1976 (see also Greenfield, 1982). Jackson's comment was sure to alienate Jews, who were an important segment of the Democratic party.

In Jackson's case, moreover, the problem was exacerbated by the candidate's handling of the situation. His reactions after the comment was made public raised doubts about his judgment and integrity. He first denied having made the comment, then said he did not recall having made it, then reversed himself and apologized for having made it. The confession and apology—in a New Hampshire synagogue on the night before the primary—were too little, too late for a candidate whose image within the Jewish community was already tarnished.

Television correspondents presented what had happened in the following ways:

Jackson's Negative Role Models . . . may even have ended his hope of becoming a party leader.

On February 27, Dan Rather summarized Jackson's daily activities by saying,

> Jackson is trying to put a lapse of memory, and some say a lapse of taste, behind him.

Later in the same broadcast, Rather introduced a filmed report from New Hampshire by saying,

> For Jesse Jackson, this is not only the night before [the New Hampshire primary] but the night after—the night after he appeared in a New Hampshire synagogue and acknowledged blame for referring to Jews as, quote, "Hymies." Jackson previously said only that he didn't remember referring to Jews with that slur. As Bob Fall reports, now that Jackson has taken the blame and apologized for what he said, the question is whether voters will forgive and forget.

Bob Fall's report quoted Jackson's critics in the following way:

> [Jackson] has put the issue on the table but he has not put it to rest. Everywhere Jackson went today, it chased him. "Why didn't you own up to the slurs sooner?" one questioner asked. Said another, "Now don't you think that in order to be consistent you should withdraw from this race?"

The tag line to Fall's report asks,

> The question remains, which will count more, Jackson's candor now or insensitivity then?

The previous day, February 26, CBS ended its film report about Jackson's apology this way:

> He still wants to meet with Jewish leaders. Today one of them said Jackson's latest charges [about an organized conspiracy to undermine his campaign] simply are not true.

Personality Roles as a whole did not help Jackson.

The substance of the reports was that the candidate had lied under pressure. As if making a politically stupid comment was not enough, he had compounded his sin by denying that he had made the comment. Few believed his initial denial, and his later admission of guilt intensified the doubts already present about his integrity.

The way the film clips were edited reinforced the substance of the reports. Their introductions emphasized questions about Jackson's candor and honesty, and their tag lines always left the viewer with a lingering doubt about that same candor and honesty. Indeed, twice in the same week CBS showed a *New York Times* advertisement headlined, ''Why would any Jew vote for Jesse Jackson? Why would any decent American?''

The entire incident shed various negative lights on the candidate. In uttering an anti-Semitic remark, Jackson offended Jews. In disregarding the special sensitivities of a religious minority, he offended civil libertarians. In seeking to deny the truth about his action, he offended moralists. To Democrats in general, Jackson's charisma turned into a negative force that made him seem exactly the opposite of what a role model ought to be.

In all, there were 43 reports that cast Jackson as a Negative Role Model. Hart had 10 and Mondale 15. The negative roles for Hart questioned his candor in reporting a name change earlier in his life, and the Mondale negative roles questioned his judgment in suggesting that Jimmy Carter's aide Bert Lance become the Democratic party chairman. (Lance had left office during the Carter years when accused of having engaged in illegal banking practices.)

The Negative Role Models that were associated with Hart and Mondale differ significantly from the ones associated with Jackson. Reporters questioned Jackson's integrity and honesty in their reports of the Hymietown incident. For Hart and Mondale, reporters challenged only the candidates' judgment. Hart may have been devious in changing his name from Hartpence to Hart, and he may have been a little embarrassed by his own ethnic origins. But those particular negative traits do not disqualify a person for high public office.[2] Similarly, Mondale may have been insensitive to public opinion by suggesting that a Jimmy Carter advisor lead the Democratic party. After all, Carter had been defeated four years earlier; Mondale's own association with the Carter administration was considered a liability; and even though Lance had been acquitted of all charges against him and had organized Mondale's successful super-Tuesday primary campaigns in Georgia and the rest of the South, he was probably best remembered for the allegations against him of illicit bank-

Television not only portrayed Jackson as having an unsuitable Personality, but it also concentrated on that Personality in a disproportionately large number of stories.

ing practices. Again, therefore, the worst that can be said is that Mondale's judgment was poor—hardly a disqualifying attribute.

But Jackson's Negative Role Models probably ended his slim hope of gaining the nomination (and may even have ended his hope of becoming a party leader). The public appearance of honesty is a necessary condition for attaining high public office. Like Mondale and Hart, Jackson found reporters challenging his judgment; but unlike his two opponents, Jackson also had reporters challenging his basic attributes of character.

This was not a media conspiracy as much as the reflection of a preconceived sense of what constitutes news during a campaign.

Personality Roles as a Whole

Personality Roles as a whole did not help Jackson. His strongest personality attributes were either ignored (sense of humor) or turned against him (hard work)—even though in one case the negative interpretation of a positive quality ultimately was shown to be invalid. His vulnerability (opportunism) was set forth in detail. His perceived weaknesses (anti-Semitism and moral irresponsibility) were made into lead stories. Thus, the Personality Roles reported for Jackson were not ones that any psychohistorian would prescribe for a would-be president.

Furthermore, Jackson received more than his fair share of stories about Personality. Twenty percent of his roles were Personality Roles—five times as many as for any other Democratic presidential candidate (see Figure 9). In effect, television not only portrayed Jackson as having an unsuitable Personality, but it also concentrated on that Personality in a disproportionately large number of stories.

This was not a media conspiracy as much as the reflection of a preconceived sense of what constitutes news during a campaign. With the horse-race metaphor considered inapplicable to Jackson's campaign, journalists searched for some other context that would give continuity and longevity to their stories about his candidacy. For a candidate who, reporters felt, surely deserved national attention but was not thought to have a chance of becoming the party's nominee, Personality Roles replaced Horse-Race Roles.

Endnotes

1. Surprisingly, research shows that among children, Watergate did not much erode this image of the benevolent leader. See Arterton, 1974; Hershey and Hill, 1975.

2. Of course, events in 1987 called Hart's integrity into question, which did disqualify him from high public office.

5. OUTSIDER ROLES

The defining characteristic of an Outsider is that he or she takes a nontraditional career path in pursuit of power. And because voters need to know whether a candidate tends to adopt or reject traditional norms of political behavior, news correspondents who assign candidates an Outsider Role (where appropriate) are fulfilling their responsibility to the public.

When a candidate is cast in the Outsider Role and shown as a person who will not abide by generally accepted political norms, he or she joins a long line of American politicians. In the Senate, for example, some members have made names for themselves by refusing to conform to the folkways of the institution (Huitt, 1961). In recent history, such senatorial mavericks as Paul Douglas of Illinois, Wayne Morse of Oregon, and (currently) William Proxmire of Wisconsin deliberately chose to depart from generally accepted political norms. They would break party ranks to vote with the opposition, oppose a president of their own party, and introduce legislation on subjects their colleagues found objectionable or politically difficult.

No institution can stand too many Outsiders, but a few nonconformists help define the standards that institutional regulars abide by. Moreover, an Outsider may be useful as a lightning rod, either taking positions that insiders sympathize with but would find it politically disadvantageous to espouse in public, or else attracting supporters who would be an embarrassment to insiders.

In the Senate, someone who takes a nontraditional career path in pursuit of power may, in the end, achieve power and be granted a place in the inner circle alongside colleagues who conformed to the institution's norms (Huitt, 1961). Among presidential candidates, however, where the inner circle consists of only one person, to flout the norms of the club is probably to be excluded from the inner circle. No Outsider presidential candidate within the past few decades has achieved his electoral goal or even become a leader in his party or had much influence on presidential politics after the campaign for

Jackson was cast in an Outsider Role more frequently . . . than any of the other four leading Democratic candidates.

the nomination. Yet all received considerable media attention for violating the accepted norms of presidential campaigning.

Outsider presidential candidates Democrat Eugene McCarthy in 1968, Republicans Pete McClosky and John Ashbrook in 1972, and Republican John Anderson in 1980 all challenged either an incumbent president of their own party or the front runner of their own party. They argued that the policies of the leadership had diverted the party from its normal course and that they, the challengers, could recapture an alienated segment of the party. Eugene McCarthy had one of the most liberal voting records in the Senate when he challenged President Johnson; McClosky and Ashbrook represented, respectively, the liberal and conservative wings of the Republican party when they challenged President Nixon; and Anderson was a moderate Republican during a conservative swing within the GOP. None of the four had national visibility before embarking on his presidential campaign, and most professional politicians initially viewed them as an embarrassment to the leadership.

In sum, Outsiders may perform an important function for the party and for the system by emphasizing forgotten issues and party positions that no one else attends to. And being cast in an Outsider Role does not necessarily harm a candidate with the voters, since nonconformity can be popular with a discontented citizenry. An Outsider can therefore be a serious candidate for president. But Outsiders also achieve little in the way of real or lasting influence.

The 1984 Campaign for the Nomination

In 1984, as one might expect, Jesse Jackson was cast in an Outsider Role more frequently (both relatively and absolutely) than any of the other four leading Democratic candidates (see Figure 11). None of the other candidates was cast in the Outsider Role more than a dozen times, but Jackson was cast in that role 76 times, or 7 percent of all the television stories in which he figured.

There were several kinds of Outsider Roles for Jackson. Sometimes he was shown as an Outsider to the party, sometimes to the American political system, and sometimes to an institution American vot-

Sometimes he was shown as an Outsider to the party, sometimes to the American political System, and sometimes to . . . the mass media.

Figure 11

Outsider Roles as Percentage of All Roles

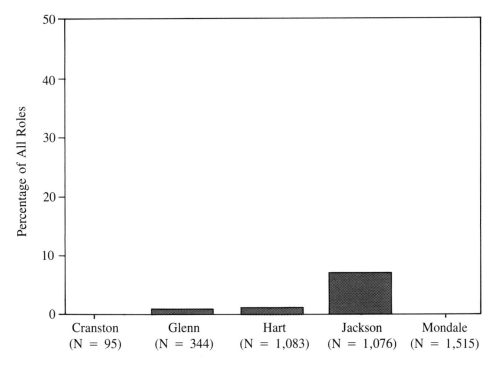

ers rely on during the campaign—the mass media. At times the roles worked to his advantage, but mostly not.

With reference to the party, some Democratic leaders supported Jackson's candidacy precisely *because* they looked on him as an Outsider and thought that as such, he would be able to help the party. The party was probably going to run a centrist campaign against Ronald Reagan—a campaign that would not appeal to either liberals or blacks. Yet the support of both those groups was thought essential to the Democrats. Some party leaders reasoned that Jackson's advocacy of traditional liberal positions could "bring home" liberals and blacks, to whom neither Reagan nor Mondale would be very attractive on election day. This reasoning worked to Jackson's advantage.

On television, however, three stories indicated that Jackson and his followers were creating dissension in the party; six times he was described as a potential "spoiler" of the chances of other Democratic hopefuls; and several other stories spoke of his refusal to promise his support to the eventual Democratic nominee. For example, he was asked before the New Hampshire primary whether he would support the Democratic party during the general election campaign if Walter Mondale was its presidential nominee. Jackson retorted that he would if Walter Mondale would make a similar pledge about a Jackson nomination. (Reporters did not follow up on Jackson's implicit suggestion that they query the party's front runner.)

Other stories described Jackson as the Democratic candidate who took an "unpopular ideological position on the left." The context of these stories was the Reagan presidency, which not only had apparent popularity with large segments of the Democratic party but also had shaped the party's agenda throughout 1984. This was the year of conservative politics—yet Jackson was talking about unemployment, social welfare programs, and racial injustice. Those issues had, to be sure, served as central themes for Democratic party politics for four decades, but 1984 was different, and Jackson's rhetoric was setting him apart from the general conservatism of that year. In this context, the Outsider Role worked to Jackson's disadvantage, even though the positions he was articulating were the ones that it was thought could attract disaffected liberals and blacks to the Democratic party.

Still other stories about Jackson's Outsider relationship to the party spoke of the minority status of black voters and mentioned that civil rights issues would probably have little appeal among the nation's white majority—the group whose votes were necessary for the Democrats to win in November.

With respect to the American political system as a whole, Jackson's playing the role of Outsider was considered both beneficial to the system and harm-

Whereas most of the speeches Jackson made in the course of a day may have been about social welfare programs, the inner cities, or unemployment, what television emphasized was his Outsider comments.

ful. The beneficial side was pointed out by a Mondale supporter, Mayor Richard Arrington of Birmingham, Alabama, in an NBC news film clip that was broadcast on March 14, 1984, the day after the Super Tuesday primaries. Arrington (who is black) was presented as saying, "What I'm hoping that Jesse will accomplish through his running is that he will get these young black voters who have been so apathetic . . . that he will find some way to keep them in the political process."

However, some stories damaged Jackson by showing him as antagonistic to the American political system. For example, 16 stories presented his criticism of the American process of selecting a presidential candidate: his attacks on the fairness of the nominating system or on the representativeness of elected convention delegates. These criticisms in themselves were no stronger than the assessments of the system that appear regularly on the editorial pages of metropolitan newspapers or in scholarly journals, but challenges to the electoral system by a losing candidate seem like sour grapes to an essentially patriotic electorate.

As an Outsider vis-a-vis the media, Jackson was shown in 11 stories to be criticizing the media's "unfair" treatment of him. In some of these stories he criticized reporters for not asking the questions he thought they should be asking, and at others he was presented as making the broader claim that the press was biased and incapable of reporting his campaign fairly.

To say that television news stories cast Jackson in an Outsider Role is not to claim that they distorted the facts about him. Indeed, 71 percent of the televised campaign news reports in this study included filmed or live reports that backed up the analysis. But whereas most of the speeches Jackson made in the course of a day may have been about social welfare programs, the inner cities, or unemployment, what television emphasized was his Outsider comments.

Selection from among several possible stories was not the only way in which television news reports emphasized Jackson's role as an Outsider. Subtle

Selection from among several possible stories was not the only way in which television news reports emphasized Jackson's role as an Outsider. Subtle broadcast production techniques achieved the same result.

broadcast production techniques achieved the same result. For example, stories that described each candidate's daily activities often mentioned Jackson last or omitted him completely. In one such story, on March 4, 1984, NBC devoted a lengthy report to Glenn, Hart, and Mondale; it followed that story with a completely separate one on Jackson's visits to southern Baptist churches. In another story, an NBC report of March 3, 1984, Jackson's campaign was almost ignored:

> Last night's dinner in Georgia featured two of the men expected to battle over the South, *along with Jesse Jackson* [emphasis added]—Mondale, with his support from organized labor and the party establishment, and John Glenn, more conservative, with a military background thought to suit this region. Now comes the wild card, the candidate of new ideas, new generation, New Hampshire. Gary Hart was not supposed to be a factor in the South.

The story is about Hart, who in fact did poorly in southern primaries, and it ignores Jackson, who in fact did well. Even though the reporter himself foreshadows Jackson's success, he downplays Jackson's significance.

With respect to Outsider Roles, then, Jackson was treated differently from his fellow Democrats. He and only he was presented as an Outsider, was assigned the role of a nontraditional player. Moreover, this role had several different layers: he was shown as a spoiler for front-running candidates, as an occasional adversary of his party leaders, and as perhaps not even a patriot. John Glenn, in withdrawing from the race, was shown criticizing the press for unfair coverage, but neither Glenn nor Cranston, Hart, or Mondale was presented as a potential defector, dissenter, non-supporter, antagonist, spoiler, or critic in relation to the American political system.

Perhaps the most interesting question of the 1984 presidential election, and possibly of American politics generally, is why Jackson's Outsider Roles were so devastating to his campaign. Why could Jackson not take advantage of being an Outsider, as presidential candidate Anderson or U.S. Senators Paul Douglas, Wayne Morse, and William Proxmire before him had done?

*B*ut for a candidate who is thought to have no chance of winning, an Outsider Role makes him (or her) seem obtrusive and brash.

The answer to that question lies in the structure of American society as reflected in television news coverage of presidential elections. Jackson was not thought to have a chance of winning, because he is black. Anderson, however slight his chances, had a probability of winning that was greater than zero because he is white. For any candidate who is considered to be in the horse race, an Outsider Role makes him (or her) seem unconventional, anomalous, and probably newsworthy. But for a candidate who is thought to have no chance of winning, an Outsider Role makes him (or her) seem obtrusive and brash. Ultimately, the fact of Jackson's race guaranteed the kind of Outsider treatment that television news gave him.

6. CONCLUSION

Television news coverage of the 1984 Democratic nominating campaign helped Jesse Jackson and it hurt him. It helped him by legitimating his candidacy; it hurt him by giving him different treatment from the treatment it gave the other potential nominees. What is more, the differences were generally not to Jackson's advantage.

When one considers the liberal democratic values upon which most American political institutions are based, it is easy to see how television news was an aid to Jackson. Television described Jackson as a democrat relatively more often than any other Democratic candidate except Cranston.Jackson was a member of, and received support from, a large tertiary group—which enhanced his image as a spokesman for a large bloc of people. His taking on the role of critic of the Republican incumbency established his credentials as a member of the loyal opposition. His articulation of issue positions created the image of him as an informed candidate. And the interest his candidacy generated among large numbers of citizens helped create the image of him as a leader of newly registered voters. In short, television news portrayed Jackson as the kind of candidate for president of the United States that American voters expect—a democrat, a participant in democratic procedures.

By showing Jackson as fully a democrat, television helped legitimate his candidacy. Even though many blacks had doubts about the *viability* of a black presidential candidate and many whites had doubts about the *desirability* of a black presidential candidate, television news was definitive about Jesse Jackson's right to be in the race. He was to receive fair treatment like any other presidential candidate because he was using established electoral procedures in an attempt to gain public office. More important than the fact that he won some primaries and lost some was the fact that he was shown as fully participating in the entire process. (Indeed, television news seemed to bend over backward to show his campaign victories and to give them as much coverage as it gave his campaign losses. As was pointed out in Chapter 2, the attention paid to his victories in primaries and cau-

Television news was definitive about Jesse Jackson's right to be in the race.

cuses was greater than one would expect, given the extent of his popularity with the electorate or with party leaders.) The image of a supporter of the constitutional framework, an adherent of the democratic regime, a believer in the structure of government itself, is an image the media bestow on all political leaders who follow the democratic rules of the game. In short, Jesse Jackson was a significant presidential candidate because he shared and acted on the values that most Americans see as underlying the nation's electoral and governmental system.

But being a significant candidate is not the same as being a potential nominee. And because television news assumed that Jackson was not a potential nominee, it set him apart—and hurt him—on the basis of the same traditional democratic values that were the underpinning of his legitimacy. For example, Jackson's Pluralism Role was closely scrutinized in media polls and interviews, whereas the other candidates received fewer references to their tertiary group support. Moreover, the Pluralism Role for Jackson conveyed a largely negative image, compounded of the antagonism of Jews, Jackson's sympathy for black militants, and the reluctance with which many black leaders supported him. In contrast, other candidates could turn their group support into a campaign asset, at least during the nomination period. (Television news did not discuss the implications of labor support for Mondale until the general election campaign.)

*B*ut being a significant candidate is not the same as being a potential nominee. And . . . television news . . . set [Jackson] apart—and hurt him—on the basis of the same traditional democratic values that were the underpinnings of his legitimacy.

A similar example of the way Democracy Roles were presented differently for Jackson (this time, however, not to his detriment), was the proportion of stories that emphasized criticism of other presidential candidates. *Within* that category, Jackson was shown to be the most loyal Democrat among the group of aspirants under consideration here (that is, he was shown proportionally more often making attacks on incumbent President Reagan and proportionally less often making attacks on his Democratic colleagues). Nevertheless, relatively fewer stories emphasized his role as partisan critic than one would expect for a candidate who was sometimes portrayed as more liberal than his Democratic colleagues.

Although in his issue positions Jackson received coverage similar to that granted to the other Democratic hopefuls, in the final Democracy Role he was again singled out (again, though, not to his detriment). He was seen as an Activator of the disaffected young black city-dwellers who had lost their faith in the Democratic party specifically and in the electoral process generally. His candidacy was expected to bring this group back into the political process, with possible payoffs for the Democratic party in the November election. These expectations, even though flattering to Jackson, were still different from the expectations held about the other candidates for the nomination.

Democracy Roles were not the only ones in which television news made Jackson seem different, to his disadvantage. Television also set him apart and hurt him in Personality Roles. Besides covering his personality far more extensively than it covered the personalities of the other leading Democratic candidates, television news emphasized his worst traits. A mission of mercy was made much of as an exercise in opportunism. A private comment about Jews became anti-Semitism, racial insensitivity, and, finally, immorality. In fact, after the early campaign news reports, most Personality Roles into which Jackson was cast displayed him as a person who, on moral and ethical grounds, was not a desirable Democratic candidate for president.

Even in its handling of Outsider Roles, television news did not enhance Jackson's candidacy. To be sure, he was occasionally presented creditably, as someone who could help keep blacks and other liberals loyal to the Democratic party and could even enlarge the numbers of blacks who took an interest in electoral politics at all. Nevertheless, he was usually presented in Outsider Roles as a dissenter, defector, antagonist, or spoiler.

The highly negative Personality and Outsider Roles in which television news cast Jackson are consistent with his low profile in news reports about the nomination campaign itself. Relatively speaking, very little attention was paid to Jackson's attempts to gain the nomination.

From the time Jackson announced his candidacy, on November 3, 1983, no one in the media thought he had a chance of succeeding in his quest. And the belief that a candidate cannot win is devastating to the coverage given his or her campaign. Journalists must abide by the norms of their profession in reporting presidential cam-

> *The highly negative Personality and Outsider Roles in which television news cast Jackson are consistent with his low profile in news reports about the nomination campaign itself.*

Television news reporters recognized that [in 1984 the United States was not ready to elect a black man as president], and their reports became a self-fulfilling prophecy **guaranteeing** *that the United States was not ready to elect a black man as president in 1984.*

paigns, and since 1960 the norm has been "horse-race journalism." In horse-race journalism, reporters focus mainly on who is winning and who is losing, and by what means. As Robert Davis (1985) has shown, since 1960 the number of news stories reporting "the means"—reporting a candidate's strategy and tactics for winning the nomination—has steadily increased (even though many media scholars lament this trend). The same increased emphasis on strategy and tactics is noticeable in televised public opinion polls, which tend more and more to focus on the horse race (Broh, 1980, 1983).

That situation explains what happened in television news coverage of Jesse Jackson. Having eliminated him in their minds from the group of possible winners, news correspondents felt little need—whether before, during, or after the trial heats and the nominating horse race itself—to investigate his tactics for winning the nomination. They also felt little need to report his victories and defeats to the same extent that they reported the other candidates' victories and defeats. There is little question that Jackson's campaign suffered as a result. For television news coverage to ignore the horse-race is equivalent to its ignoring the horse. Being left out of the race is tantamount to being ignored entirely.

Why did the media not include Jackson in the horse race? Why was he not viewed as being in contention for the nomination? The answers to these questions are multifaceted and complex, but one factor is paramount: in 1984 the United States was not ready to elect a black man as president. Television news reporters recognized this, and their reports became a self-fulfilling prophecy *guaranteeing* that the United States was not ready to elect a black man as president in 1984. They followed the horse race closely, but they knew that Jesse Jackson was not a front runner, not a contender, and not even a long shot: he was "a horse of a different color."

7. EPILOGUE

As the 1988 presidential election approaches, it is natural to consider the implications of this research for Jesse Jackson or for any other black person who may seek the presidency.[1] Five implications in particular stand out.

First, black candidates for the presidency will have to overcome the media's stereotypes. Campaign reporters explain politics with cliches, and a black presidential candidate will have to learn to confront, or to manage, those stereotypes. For example, if black leaders are divided on the question of a given black presidential candidate, the candidate can expect television news to report that he or she is politically weak—even though no one expects whites to be unified on their candidate of choice. For another example, a black presidential candidate can expect television news to report that he or she is insensitive toward Jews if he or she is, or seems to be, sympathetic to Arab nations whenever American policy in the Middle East is discussed. A successful black presidential candidate will have to figure out how to handle, if not avoid, those and comparable situations without alienating his or her black constituency.

Second, black candidates for the presidency will have to develop a strategy for receiving support from black leaders who are unpopular with white moderates. The rhetoric of some black leaders may strengthen the bonds within the black community but only at the cost of alienating many whites. Television news thrives on that kind of tension, which has all the attributes of a good news story (people, conflict, timeliness). In effect, the black candidate will be associated with the black militant unless the campaign can effectively address the matter of black supporters who are unpopular with whites.

*B*lack candidates for the presidency will have to overcome the media's stereotypes.

Third, although gaffes and blunders are a danger in any campaign, they are particularly destructive in a campaign that initially seems to lack widespread popular support. No one thought Jimmy Carter should quit in 1976 when he used the phrase ''ethnic purity,'' and Ronald Reagan survived a slur on Italian Americans in

1980. Jesse Jackson, however, found a disparaging comment about Jews to be devastating in 1984. A candidate who is trying to gain credibility can expect to feel the wrath of the media for any such inappropriate comment.

Fourth, deteriorating relations with Jewish leaders present a continuing problem for black presidential candidates. Quite simply, both groups are essential to a Democratic victory. Jews are active as contributors to, and participants in, political campaigns, and they are strategically located in important industrial states. Blacks are also strategically located in important electoral states and are more numerous than other non-white racial groups. Without cooperation between these two important minorities, no black candidate can expect television news to ignore the highly emotional issues that often separate blacks and Jews. Cooperation is particularly difficult when the Middle East dominates Americans' concerns—which it is likely to do for many years to come.

Fifth, only black candidates who follow traditional paths of leadership recruitment can expect television coverage that is undifferentiated from the coverage given white candidates. Black candidates who have not followed traditional paths toward the nomination and therefore do not really have a chance to win it will not have "typical" stories told about their candidacies. Obviously, there is a Catch-22 quality to this situation. Only possible nominees get "typical" stories—but unless television reports typical stories, a black candidate will not become a possible nominee.

Perhaps the only black candidate able to break that cycle will be someone who has regular party credentials and is not suspect as a "black" candidate. Such a person might attract the support of a loyal black constituency while having the additional party strength necessary for attracting large numbers of white voters. Then television reporters would believe the candidate had a chance to win, and media coverage would fit the traditional pattern of campaign journalism.

In sum, 1984 provides several lessons for future black politicians who seek a major-party presidential nomination. Perhaps the most important lesson of all is that tele-

Television is as formidable an obstacle as are the party's rules and procedures themselves.

vision is as formidable an obstacle as are the party's
rules and procedures themselves.

Endnotes

1. In a nationwide survey conducted in August
1986, respondents were asked about their support
for a 1988 presidential bid by Jackson. For a presentation and discussion of the findings, see Harris
and Williams, 1986.

WORKS CITED

American Political Science Association. 1950. *Toward a More Responsible Two-Party System*. Washington, D.C.: American Political Science Association.

Arterton, F. Christopher. 1974. "The Impact of Watergate on Children's Attitudes Toward Political Authority," *Political Science Quarterly* 89 (June): 269–288.

―――. 1978. "The Media Politics of Presidential Campaigns." In *The Race for the Presidency*, edited by James David Barber. Englewood Cliffs, N.J.: Prentice-Hall.

―――. 1984. *Media Politics*. Lexington, Mass.: Lexington Books.

Barber, James David. 1972. *The Presidential Character*. Englewood Cliffs, N.J.: Prentice-Hall.

―――. 1977. *The Presidential Character*. 2d ed. Englewood Cliffs, N.J.: Prentice-Hall.

Berelson, Bernard, Paul F. Lazarsfeld, and William N. McPhee. 1954. *Voting*. Chicago: University of Chicago Press.

Brady, Henry E., and Michael G. Hagen. 1986. "The 'Horse-Race' or the Issues?" Paper presented at the annual meeting of the American Political Science Association, Washington, D.C.

Broh, C. Anthony. 1980. "Horse-race Journalism," *Public Opinion Quarterly* 44:514–529.

―――. 1983. "Polls, Pols and Parties," *Journal of Politics* 45 (August): 732–744.

Campbell, Angus, Philip E. Converse, Warren E. Miller, and Donald E. Stokes. 1960. *The American Voter*. New York: John Wiley & Sons.

Carmines, Edward G., and James A. Stimson. 1980. "The Two Faces of Issue Voting," *American Political Science Review,* 74:78–91.

Cavanagh, Thomas E., and Lorn S. Foster. 1984. *Jesse Jackson's Campaign: The Primaries and Caucuses.* Washington, D.C.: Joint Center for Political Studies.

Converse, Philip E. 1964. "The Nature of Belief Systems in Mass Publics." In *Ideology and Discontent,* edited by David Apter. Glencoe, Ill.: The Free Press.

Dahl, Robert A. 1961. *Who Governs?* New Haven: Yale University Press.

Davis, Robert J. 1985. "A National Circus: Trends in Newspaper Coverage of Eight Presidential Elections." Junior Paper, Department of Politics, Princeton University.

Delli Carpini, Michael X. 1984. "Scooping the Voters? The Consequences of the Networks' Early Call of the 1980 Presidential Race." *Journal of Politics* 46 (August): 866–885.

Easton, David, and Jack Dennis. 1969. *Children in the Political System.* New York: McGraw-Hill.

Edelman, Murray. 1967. *Symbolic Uses of Politics.* Urbana: University of Illinois Press.

Faw, Bob, and Nancy Skelton. 1986. *Thunder in America.* Austin: Texas Monthly Press.

Gandy, Oscar H., Jr., and Larry G. Coleman. 1986. "The Jackson Campaign: Mass Media and Black Student Perceptions," *Journalism Quarterly* 3 (Spring): 138–143, 154.

Greenfield, Jeff. 1982. *The Real Campaign.* New York: Summit Books.

Greenstein, Fred I. 1965. *Children and Politics.* New Haven: Yale University Press.

———. 1982. *The Hidden-Hand Presidency.* New York: Basic Books, 1982.

Harris, Fredrick, and Linda Williams. 1986. "JCPS/ Gallup Poll Reflects Changing Views on Political Issues," *Focus* 14 (October): 3–7.

Hershey, Marjorie Randon, and David B. Hill. 1975. "Watergate and Preadults' Attitudes Toward the President," *American Journal of Political Science* 19 (November): 703–726.

Hess, Robert and Judith Torney. 1967. *The Development of Political Attitudes in Children*. New York: Aldine.

Hofstetter, Richard. 1976. *Bias in the News*. Columbus: Ohio State University Press.

Huitt, Ralph. 1961. "The Outsider in the Senate: An Alternative Role," *American Political Science Review* 55 (June): 333–344.

Hunter, Floyd. 1953. *Community Power Structures*. Chapel Hill: University of North Carolina Press.

Keeter, Scott, and Cliff Zukin. 1983. *Uninformed Choice*. New York: Praeger.

Key, V. O., Jr. 1966. *The Responsible Electorate*. Cambridge: Harvard University Press, Belknap Press.

Lengle, James I. 1981. *Representation and Presidential Primaries*. Westport, Conn.: Greenwood Press.

Matthews, Donald R. 1960. *U.S. Senators and Their World*. Chapel Hill: University of North Carolina Press.

McClosky, Herbert. 1964. "Consensus and Ideology in American Politics," *American Political Science Review* 58 (June): 361–382.

Milavsky, J. Ronald, Al Swift, Burns W. Roper, Richard Salant, and Floyd Abrams. 1985. "Early Calls on Election Results and Exit Polls: Pros, Cons, and Constitutional Considerations," *Public Opinion Quarterly* 49 (Spring): 1–18.

Mueller, John E. 1973. *Wars, Presidents and Public Opinion*. New York: John Wiley & Sons.

Niemi, Richard G., and Herbert F. Weisberg. 1976. *Controversies in Voting Behavior*. New York: W. H. Freeman.

———. 1984. *Controversies in Voting Behavior*. 2d ed. Washington, D.C.: Congressional Quarterly Press.

Patterson, Thomas E. 1980. *The Mass Media Election*. New York: Praeger Special Studies.

Polsby, Nelson W. 1963. *Community Power and Political Theory*. New Haven: Yale University Press.

———. 1983. *Consequences of Party Reform*. Oxford: Oxford University Press.

Ranney, Austin. 1954. *The Doctrine of Responsible Party Government*. Urbana: University of Illinois Press.

———. 1975. *Curing the Mischiefs of Faction*. Berkeley: University of California Press.

———. 1978. *The Federalization of Presidential Primaries*. Washington, D.C.: American Enterprise Institute.

Reed, Adolph L., Jr. 1986. *The Jesse Jackson Phenomenon*. New Haven: Yale University Press.

Rivers, William L. 1982. *The Other Government*. New York: Universe Press.

Robinson, Michael, Nancy Conover, and Margaret Sheehan. 1980. "The Media at Mid-Year: A Bad Year for McLuhanites?" *Public Opinion* 3 (June/July): 41–45.

Rubin, Richard L. 1981. *Press, Party and Presidency*. New York: Norton.

Salmore, Stephen A., and Barbara G. Salmore. 1985. *Candidates, Parties, and Campaigns*. Washington, D.C.: Congressional Quarterly Press.

Steeper, Frederick T. 1978. "Public Response to Gerald Ford's Statements on Eastern Europe in the Second Debate." In *The Presidential Debates*, edited by George F. Bishop, Robert G. Meadow, and Marilyn Jackson-Beek. New York: Praeger.

Sudman, Seymour. 1986. "Do Exit Polls Influence Voting Behavior?" *Public Opinion Quarterly* 50 (Fall): 331–339.

Tannenbaum, Percy H., and Leslie J. Kostrich. 1983. *Turned-On TV/Turned-Off Voters*. Beverly Hills: Sage Publications.

Turner, Julius. 1950. *Party and Constituency*. Baltimore: Johns Hopkins University Press.

White, Theodore. 1961. *The Making of the President 1960*. New York: Atheneum.

―――. 1965. *The Making of the President 1964*. New York: Atheneum.

―――. 1969. *The Making of the President 1968*. New York: Atheneum.

―――. 1973. *The Making of the President 1972*. New York: Atheneum.

Wilkins, Roger. 1985. Address to the Woodrow Wilson School, Princeton University, Princeton, New Jersey, October 4, 1985.

Witcover, Jules. 1977. *Marathon: The Pursuit of the Presidency*. New York: Viking.

ABOUT THE AUTHOR

C. Anthony Broh has written several monographs and articles about presidential elections and news coverage of political campaigns. He received his Ph.D. from the University of Wisconsin and was a post-doctoral fellow at Yale University. Currently he is Registrar for Princeton University and a Lecturer of Politics at Princeton.

SELECTED JCPS
PUBLICATIONS

Black Elected Officials: A National Roster, 1987, 16th edition.
ISSN 0882–1593. $29.50.

Black Employment in City Government, 1973-1980, Peter Eisinger, 1983. ISBN 0-941410-32-3. $4.95

Blacks on the Move: A Decade of Demographic Change,
William P. O'Hare, Jane-yu Li, Roy Chatterjee, and
Margaret Shukur, abridged by Phillip Sawicki, 1982.
ISBN 0-941410-25-0. $4.95.

The Changing Patterns of Black Family Income, 1960-1982,
Henry E. Felder, 1984. ISBN 0-941410-43-9. $4.95.

Elected and Appointed Black Judges in the United States,
1986. ISSN 0889-3179. $10.00.

Focus, JCPS monthly newsletter. ISSN 0740-0195. $15.00 per
annum.

Foreign Trade Policy and Black Economic Advancement: Pro-
ceedings of a JCPS Roundtable, 1981. ISBN
0-941410-19-6. $4.95

A Horse of a Different Color: Television's Treatment of Jesse
Jackson's 1984 Presidential Campaign, C. Anthony Broh,
1987. ISBN 0–941410–54–4. $7.95.

How to Use Section 5 of the Voting Rights Act, third edition,
Barbara Y. Phillips, 1984. ISBN 0-941410-27-7. $4.95.

Inside Black America: The Message of the Black Vote in the
1984 Elections, Thomas E. Cavanagh, 1986. ISBN
0-941410-47-1. $4.95.

The JCPS Congressional District Fact Book (1986 edition),
compiled by JCPS staff, 1986. ISSN 0888-8957. $6.95.

Minorities and the Labor Market: Twenty Years of Misguided
Policy, Richard McGahey and John Jeffries, 1985. ISBN
0-941410-53-6. $5.95.

Minority Vote Dilution, edited by Chandler Davidson, 1984.
Available from Howard University Press, 2900 Van
Ness St., Washington, DC 20008. $24.95.

Mobilizing the Black Community: The Effects of Personal Con-
tact Campaigning on Black Voters, Paul Carton, 1984.
ISBN 0-941410-42-0. $4.95.

The Nineteen Eighties: Prologue and Prospect, Kenneth B.
Clark and John Hope Franklin, 1981. ISBN
0-941410-20-X. $2.95.

A Policy Framework for Racial Justice (statement by 30 black
scholars), 1983. Introduction by Kenneth B. Clark and
John Hope Franklin. ISBN 0-941410-30-7. $4.95.

A Policy Framework for Racial Justice (II): Black Initiative and
Governmental Responsibility, 1987. Introduction by John
Hope Franklin and Eleanor Holmes Norton. ISBN 0-
941410-61-7. $6.95.

Public School Desegregation in the United States, 1968-1980,
Gary Orfield, 1983. ISBN 0-941410-29-3. $4.95.

Race and Political Strategy, edited by Thomas E. Cavanagh, 1983. ISBN 0-941410-33-1. $4.95.

Strategies for Mobilizing Black Voters: Four Case Studies, edited by Thomas E. Cavanagh, 1987. ISBN 0–941410–48–X. $8.95.

Thirty Years after Brown, Jennifer L. Hochschild, 1985. ISBN 0-941410-49-8. $4.95.

Trends, Prospects, and Strategies for Black Economic Progress, Andrew Brimmer, 1985. ISBN 0-941410-56-0. $5.95.

Wealth and Economic Status: A Perspective on Racial Inequity, William P. O'Hare, 1983. ISBN 0-941410-35-8. $4.95.